Exam Success

Exam Success

David McIlroy

SAGE Publications
London ● Thousand Oaks ● New Delhi

© David McIlroy 2005

First published 2005

Apart from any fair dealing for the purposes of research or
private study, or criticism or review, as permitted under
the Copyright, Designs and Patents Act, 1988, this publication
may be reproduced, stored or transmitted in any form, or
by any means, only with the prior permission in writing of
the publishers, or in the case of reprographic reproduction,
in accordance with the terms of licences issued by the
Copyright Licensing Agency. Inquiries concerning
reproduction outside those terms should be sent to
the publishers.

 SAGE Publications Ltd
1 Oliver's Yard
55 City Road
London EC1Y 1SP

SAGE Publications Inc.
2455 Teller Road
Thousand Oaks, California 91320

SAGE Publications India Pvt Ltd
B-42, Panchsheel Enclave
Post Box 4109
New Delhi 110 017

British Library Cataloguing in Publication data

A catalogue record for this book is available
from the British Library

ISBN 0-7619-5164-4
ISBN 0-7619-5165-2 (pbk)

Library of Congress Control Number available

Typeset by C&M Digitals (P) Ltd., Chennai, India
Printed in Great Britain by Cromwell Press Ltd, Trowbridge, Wiltshire

Contents

Introduction

Every individual who has been to school has first-hand experience of exams and knows that exams are part of the territory associated with education. Familiarity with exams, however, is not a guarantee that students will have learned either to bring their exam stress under control, or to do justice to their abilities and efforts within the short time frame allocated to exams. Moreover, exam performance can make a substantial difference to overall grades, and therefore to the breadth of available job and career opportunities.

In the nine chapters that lie ahead, a range of strategies and techniques are presented that will enable you to develop your skills and improve your level of achievement. The book is presented in a readable style and is characterised from start to finish with examples, illustrations, bullet points, headings and exercises. The exercises are designed to make the learning material interactive, so that you will not merely be a passive recipient of information.

The illustrations and examples are drawn from concepts that all students will be familiar with to a greater or lesser extent. These include music, personal relationships, travel, education and films. There are also many minor examples to complement these and it is hoped that you will find these interesting and beneficial. The challenge is to take the principles presented in these examples and illustrations and to use them in relation to your own subject area. Given that the examples and illustrations are drawn from common experience and everyday affairs, these should provide you with a ready reference point on which to build and from which to transfer your acquired skills to your own subject area.

The chapters that are covered in this book deal with personal characteristics such as motivation, confidence and anxiety control. Attention to these personal features can enable you to function at your best both in preparation for and performance in an exam. *The important message that underlies this book is that you can break away from past habits – no matter how entrenched they may have become.* You are pointed to clear strategies and techniques that will help you get to grips with learning, revision, planning and organisation. There are sections to direct you to best time and task management, and you will be stimulated to think of what examiners look for, and how you should read exam questions.

One chapter is devoted to memory techniques and you will learn how to make the most efficient use of your memory. However, there is repeated emphasis on 'deep' as opposed to 'shallow' learning, and therefore memory work is advocated as the starting point. Current educational principles are recurrent themes in the book and these include key and core skills, employability qualities, transferable skills, critical thinking and problem-based learning. There is also emphasis on quality note-taking and the ability to alternate in revision between reading extended material and using effective summary points. You will also be challenged to apply, illustrate and structure your material in a manner that will enable you to process your information at a higher level of understanding.

A unique feature of this book is a series of diagnostic tests in the form of exercises that you can score yourself, through the use of objective performance indicators, to pinpoint your own strengths and weaknesses. This will allow you to have more than a vague feeling about these and should empower you to sharpen and shape your awareness of the direction you will need to take. Most of these were designed for the book and you can use them as a reference point to measure your habits, behaviours, attitude, personal discipline, etc. Given that the measures highlight personal issues, and that you can complete them in total secrecy, you can therefore be totally honest with yourself on both your negative and positive attributes.

However, the exercises are not designed to be tedious so you should not get hung up on them. You could decide, for example, to spend just a minute or two on each one and then move on so that you do not lose the fluency of the chapter. If you are working through the exercises as a group, you may decide to spend a little longer than the above guidelines on some that you select for more intense activity. The aim is to give you a flavour of the kinds of things you should address in order to give yourself the best opportunity to refine your study skills and exam techniques. Do not worry if you feel that you are inadequate after some of the exercises. As you read further into the book you will become more aware of the factors that are likely to boost your confidence, lessen your anxiety and improve your motivation.

If you look at the contents list of this book you will find that the first chapters seem to relate to tackling all types of assessment work. And you would be right to query whether all this really will contribute to your success in exams. It will! This book will help you to see that your overall approach to assessment and learning in your course work will undoubtedly affect your exam performance – it's not all down to end-of-term revision and exam technique. When you walk into the exam room you will 'carry' with you not just the results of the time of revision prior to the exams, but the skills and knowledge that you have acquired over your entire university experience.

In conclusion, the earlier you start to incorporate the strategies and techniques presented in the book the sooner you will see the positive impact on your results. However, there are no quick and easy solutions to entrenched problems, but you can gradually introduce effective changes, as you are able. It is emphasised that exams do not stand independently in the educational system, and therefore cannot be approached in isolation from other aspects of your academic assessment. The exam-related skills you develop will have positive knock-on effects for other aspects of your academic programme and vice versa. Over the full course of your academic programme you will observe positive changes in both strategy and performance. The skills you learn will not only spread across your academic programme and over its duration, but will also extend into your future career.

1 Overview

1.1   Something old, something new

If you have not yet commenced your course at university or college, you will no doubt already have faced a number of tests and exams, and their nature will not be totally new to you. Some of the features of exams that will be familiar, either from or before your third-level education, are:

- A formal setting with strict rules

- A set time and place

- Invigilators to ensure rules are observed

- Rigidly observed times to start and finish

- An exam paper that you will see just before the test begins

- Quietness – except for pen on paper!

These features will generally remain the same in third-level education, so that you are not going to have to navigate entirely new terrain. Indeed, some of the major differences may lie in your own perceptions rather than in objective criteria. However, some characteristics that might be different from your previous experience are:

- An overall increase in the number of tests

- A shorter duration between the tests

- Shorter time frames in which to prepare for tests

- The length of the tests themselves

- A different emphasis on what is required (more critical, less descriptive)

- Larger numbers of students in the test room

These features may vary from one university to the next, and your overall impression may be different from your previous test experience. Nevertheless, it will help you if you can see the parallels and identify the common threads.

It is easier to step into the unknown if you can find some familiar ground to stand on.

In all of life you have to face things that are unfamiliar. However, on closer inspection you are likely to find common features between the old and the new. An example would be the use of the public transport system in another city or town. Some other examples are:

- Going to a new restaurant

- Shopping at a new supermarket

- Operating a new system at your bank

- Driving a car with controls in different places

- Using a different currency in another country (e.g. on holiday)

What you do in each of these cases is that you use the familiar to develop the unfamiliar.

Exercise — See if you can write your own checklist that identifies some of the exam-related skills that you have used before and will need to use again.

✓ Making a quick decision about the questions to tackle

✓ ....

✓ ....

✓ ....

✓ ....

Some of the skills you may have thought of would probably include: working out the time to spend on each question and on each section of a question; writing out the outline points and arranging these into the preferred order; making note of any important names associated with the topic; strategies to handle anxious reactions.

1.2 Using the decision-making process

There are many aspects of academic life in which you will be forced to be decisive. Although no one is standing directly over you to threaten or accuse, it is always as if a gentle authority is spurring you on to be decisive. Part of your academic training is about learning to make decisions and to be decisive. You may not particularly like making decisions until you are on the brink of the expiry date for you time limit! By all means get all the information you can to help you make your choice, but remember the joke about 'I used to be indecisive, but now I am not so sure!'

An aim of this book is to assist you in making informed choices, and to make decisions that will minimise your anxiety, maximise your motivation, confidence and planning, and facilitate the development of your skills and potential.

Decisions that you have already made may include:

• **To enter college or university**

• **Study full-time or part-time**

- **Choice of study programme**

- **Study away from or near home**

- **Movement towards a chosen career**

- **To find employment outside your studies (either full-time or part-time)**

Decisions that may have yet to be made:

- **Ratio of academic work to social life**

- **Choice of modules to study**

- **Choice of topics for revision**

- **Choice of study strategies**

- **Choice of note-taking methods**

- **Study at home or college (or mixed)**

- **Time allocation for each subject**

- **Time allocation to each learning activity**

1.3 Two different animals — course work and exams?

Checklist — the similarities between course work and exams

✓ Both require structure and planning
✓ Both must address the set question
✓ Supportive evidence must be presented in both

Checklist — the differences between course work and exams

- ✓ In course work there is plenty of time to correct mistakes
- ✓ In exams you must stick to a very strict time limit
- ✓ In course work you can experiment before deciding on the final structure

Now you can think of the skills required to produce a competent piece of course work (the direction of the arrows indicate that the five factors contribute to the quality of the finished product).

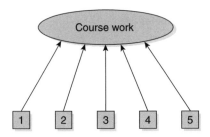

The five points above could be identified (from left to right as):

1. Ability to focus on and address the question   ....

2. Use of relevant background research   ....

3. Working for balance and structure in arguments   ....

4. Maintaining a clear and succinct style throughout   ....

5. Providing a useful introduction and conclusion   ....

Exercise — Now go back and put a tick on the dotted lines of the five points above if you are convinced that these points can also be applied to exams.

You may have concluded that all of the five points are useful for exams, and you would be right. The one additional skill that is unique to exams is time management under pressure – there is less time to complete your task and no luxury of experimenting with ideas that can later be deleted or moved to another place on your script. So take your course work skills into the exam room and apply them effectively by good use of time.

1.4   The issue of IQ

Much debate has gone into the definition and usefulness of intelligence over many decades (Cooper, 1999). It has traditionally been seen to include factors such as verbal reasoning, mathematical and logical ability, and spatial/mechanical competence. Another important element is deemed to be the speed in which problems can be solved. Early theorists suggested that intelligence incorporates the capacity to adapt to one's environment and to survive within it (Sternberg, 1996). This accounts for the value placed on abilities within a given culture (such as spearing a fish or navigating a canoe around an island by the stars). It is argued that rigid, traditional concepts stifle the potential and gifts of young children who are 'short changed' by the educational system. It is said that exams are more of a test of ability than other forms of assessment because of the time/speed factor required. However, some individuals may produce high-quality work if the pressure of time is removed from them.

Howard Gardner (1983) came up with the model of multiple intelligences that include both traditional features such as verbal/linguistic, visual/spatial, logical/mathematical skills, and additional features such as bodily/kinaesthetic, musical, interpersonal and intrapersonal (self-knowledge skills). You may wish to rate yourself on each of these seven intelligences (Gardner has more recently added a few other factors to these basic seven). The exercise in the Appendix will help you to do this and you may wish to tackle this now or when you have finished this chapter.

The emphasis throughout this book is on both the refinement of your abilities and on the development and deployment of your personal qualities.

1.5   Exams: a tug-of-war for their future

Some educationalists argue for the eventual removal of exams from the educational system. Some of these arguments are:

- **Exams encourage surface learning (cramming)**

- **What is learned is too quickly forgotten**

- Good students might underachieve because of recurrent problems with test anxiety

- Students may work hard only around exam times

- Sustained symptoms from anxiety are not beneficial to anyone

On the other hand, arguments for course work are:

- Course work encourages deeper learning

- It promotes learning that lasts in the memory

- It gives students time to organise structure and presentation

- Students have the opportunity to experiment with various formats

- Students receive feedback that can be diagnostic and formative

However, many educationalists argue that the total removal of exams is impractical and counterproductive. Some of the advantages associated with exams are:

- Plagiarism is reduced or eliminated

- Students get experience of testing situations for their future career

- Exams provide an opportunity to respond quickly to set problems

- Exams are an opportunity to demonstrate a range of unique skills

There has been a move in many third-level institutions to reduce the number of exams in the study programmes and to develop a full range of assessment methods (documented later in the chapter). At the present it looks like exams are here to stay within third-level education, although they will be used alongside an increasing variety of complementary assessment methods. From the standpoint of staff, it is difficult to provide quality feedback for students at a personal level where there are large student numbers and staff/student ratios are high. The retention of exams helps to reduce this problem, especially in environments where numbers in third-level education has dramatically increased over several decades. For you as a student, it is important that you are clear about the assessment criteria of your study programme, and if these are likely to be changed during the course of your academic career.

1.6 Handy hints on planning your assessment schedules

A simple and practical piece of advice to keep your assessment tasks always in view is to use a wall chart. You can then add information about course work deadlines, exam times and venues etc., and you can arrange this in order so that you can quickly see which assessment comes next, which ones are close together in time, and then you can make your plans without last-minute panic.

In addition, it will be useful for you to:

- Make sure you receive and regularly consult a handbook where assessment methods are mapped out for the duration of the academic year

- Watch for any changes that are made at any stage of your programme and make careful note of these (i.e. not on scrap paper!)

- Check and update your revision plans as they may necessitate more detailed planning of revision stages

- Ensure that you plan to keep all your work up to date, especially where there are competing pressures from modules running in parallel

- Beware of using redundant course handbooks after changes have been made

- Watch out for assessments that are scheduled for submission around the same time, and plan well for these

- Check if exams are balanced between semesters or are all at the end of one semester

- Check if modules last for one semester or are year-long

- Ascertain dates, times and venues for exams as soon as these are known

- Attach copies of your assessment programme to your study folders so that you can maintain a clear and accurate picture regularly

- Maintain awareness of course work deadlines and plan work accordingly

Illustration – A mind map for the city

If you move to live in a new city it will be important for you to get your bearings as soon as possible. Perhaps the initial strategy would be to obtain a one-page map of the city centre so that you can carry it around with you and quickly locate where you are at a glance. Alternatively, you can simply ask directions, although you cannot always be certain that these will be accurate, and this approach is only a short-term solution. Failure to acquire a mental map of the city will lead to time wasting, frustration, anxiety and walking in circles! When you acquire some familiarity with a few streets and landmarks, these small beginnings will make all the difference to your exercises in orienteering!

In the same way you should build up a picture in your mind of the number, nature and timing of your academic assessments so that you can carefully plan and pace your learning activities, revision strategy and your management of time and tasks.

A wise old gentleman used to say that a cheap article, such as a pair of cheap shoes, could be an expensive purchase in the long run. The idea was that if the item was of poor quality you would need to replace it a number of times over the same duration that a quality article would remain intact. Remember then to stop and pay the full price for learning about the facts of your assessments. If you only remember about these when you are about to be overtaken by them, the 'cheap option' will prove to be too expensive.

1.7 Outlining the advantages

It is always better to light a candle as curse the darkness.

If exams are a frequent element in your programme, then resolve to benefit from them as much as possible. In order to avoid the shallow learning that educationalists warn of, you can prepare for your exams by beginning to learn the material well in advance.

As a result of this planned approach to learning, you will deposit your learning in more permanent storage and may be able to carry it on for further use at later stages of your study programme.

Exam advantages – what exams will give you:

- **Revision strategies and exam techniques that you will be able to use again and again**

- **The ability to work economically under strict time limits**

- **The capacity to respond efficiently to an immediate challenge that is set before you**

- **A sharpened focus on a new task that is set before you**

- **The ability to filter your learning through set questions**

- **The competence to draft short, quick outline plans**

- **Control over your thoughts and emotions**

- **Confidence so that you can face fresh and demanding challenges**

- **Efficiency in combining time and task management**

In short, exams will help you to develop and refine the kinds of quality that are required in many vocations and that many employers value. It may be that in your chosen occupation you will need to work under time pressure and think clearly 'on your feet'. You may at times be required to justify at short notice the stewardship of your responsibilities to your bosses. This may entail crystallising your major character strengths and abilities and presenting them in short, sharp, summary points. If you cultivate the strategies advocated throughout this book, you will acquire the capacity to maximise your efficiency in exams and develop your potential in the world of work.

It will help your approach to exams if you see them as not merely occasions to 'regurgitate' what you have learned, but as opportunities to develop life-long skills that you will use repeatedly.

Checklist — In order to maintain a positive frame of mind about exams, it may be helpful to document some of the benefits (short-term and/or long-term) that exams will bring to you.

- ✓ An ability to respond quickly to a set task or problem
- ✓ An ability to work under pressure
- ✓ A capacity to focus intensely on a specific task
- ✓ An awareness of how to turn anxiety to your advantage
- ✓ The confidence to apply your skills to similar future tasks

1.8 Profiling some general exam-related problems

It may at first glance seem strange to profile the problems of exams immediately after a section that was designed to help you form a positive frame of mind. However, the way to achieve a positive and productive approach to exams is not by denying reality, but by facing up to the problems and by 'taking the bull by the horns'. As a result of a head-on approach, you can either bring exam-related problems under control or put them into proper perspective. These general points will give you an initial feel for problems that are addressed more thoroughly in subsequent chapters.

PROBLEM 1 — TEST ANXIETY

Test anxiety has been found to impair students' test or exam performance (see later discussion). On the positive side, though, test anxiety is not intractable and can be reduced, and when this happens performance improves (Hembree, 1988). Chapter 5 will alert you to strategies for controlling test anxiety and channelling the nervous energy into productive activity. For the present, you can prepare yourself by suggesting a few factors that you have already used to control exam anxiety.

1. ....

2. ....

3. ....

PROBLEM 2 – AFTER THE HORSE HAS BOLTED

When an exam is over, you do not get a chance to go back and correct the mistakes you have made. Neither can you solicit anyone to read over your script to correct the 'howlers' before you submit your exam paper. If you later become aware of a mistake you made in an exam, this can become a trigger for intense worry. Often the problems are not as big as they seem.

Illustration – Coins obscuring a mountain

Two small coins held immediately in front of your eyes are big enough at that point to block out the view of a large mountain that stands immediately in front of you. Students sometimes get so obsessed with the small mistakes they have made and fail to focus on the mountain of quality work that they have managed to produce.

PROBLEM 3 – FEEDBACK FROM EXAMS

The problem with feedback from exams is that there often is none! Or, if feedback is given, it may be to the whole group and is therefore general rather than specific. Students sometimes complain that they do not know where they are going wrong in exams, and do not always have the benefit of individual feedback. Some tutors may provide summaries of the exam performance of previous cohorts of students, and these will identify recurrent problems to be avoided. These are the kinds of problem that are identified in this book, and the purpose of the subsequent chapters will be to:

- **Identify the most common exam shortcomings**

- **Provide diagnostic tests for you to trace your own weaknesses**

- Highlight useful exam strategies to help you take pre-emptive action

- Set exercises that will help you stretch to work harder and smarter

PROBLEM 4 – FEELING OF ISOLATION

In an exam you may feel alone and isolated and you may look around and feel that almost everyone else is cool, calm and collected. Do not be deceived by this as there is always a substantial percentage of students that suffer from exam nerves.

Illustration – Like ducks to water?

The host complemented a woman contestant on a television quiz show for her apparent calmness in tackling questions, as large sums of money were at stake. She replied that he should not be fooled by this calm appearance, as she felt like a duck – calm in appearance above the surface of the water, but a lot of vigorous paddling under the water! So if you imagine that all the other students have taken to their exam tasks 'like ducks to the water', then remember this woman's words!

In order to help your confidence in an exam, you should remember that:

- Others will feel exactly like you

- Your fellow students are doing the same test, at the same time, under the same conditions

- Others will be thinking similar task-related thoughts as you, for example, reflect on times of group learning when agreed conclusions were reached

- Tests are of very short duration and will quickly be over

- When in the exam room focus primarily on the test itself and do not let your thoughts stray

The problems highlighted above are general and are primarily psychological in nature. The remainder of the book will focus on practice, habits, strategies and techniques for learning, thinking and exam performance. However, such issues as motivation, confidence and anxiety control are also addressed.

1.9   Role of tests in the educational system

Some educationalists have asserted that assessment should be designed to include both process and product. In other words, it is not just what you produce as an end result that matters (such as in an exam), but what you have gone through in the learning activities and processes that lead up to that point.

At this stage of the chapter you should now be clear that exams are more than a test of knowledge and memory. Quality control bodies encourage third-level academic institutions to produce a variety of assessment methods and to develop innovative approaches to assessing students. Exams themselves can take on various appearances, including:

- Seen and unseen questions

- Multiple choice

- Computer-based tests

- A series of short answer questions

- An oral component (e.g. a viva)

An exam may not always be presented to you in the more traditional form, but variety does not guarantee that your anxiety will be lessened.

In addition to the various types of exam referred to above, other forms of assessment may include:

- Course work essays

- Lab reports

- Experiments

- Surveys

- Presentations

- Field projects

- Work-based learning

- Portfolios

Part of the rationale behind this is that students who have weaknesses in particular forms of assessment (such as exams) will not be severely disadvantaged in their potential to achieve. Although this ethos should help to take some of the pressure from exams, they are still a very important component of overall assessment. However, if you do well in your other forms of assessment this may help your exam confidence and will also equip you with skills that are useful in exams.

1.10   Play to your strengths

Illustration – The coach with the game plan

In the game of cricket it is normal practice to put in the best and strongest batsmen early in the batting order. The middle-order batsmen come next and then the weakest at the tail end follow these. In order to determine the rank order in batting, it is probable that previous batting average is taken into account. The weakest batsmen are in the team because they have other qualities, such as good skills at fielding, running, catching, fast bowling, spin bowling and wicket keeping. Some players may be good at playing for time to obtain a draw when a win is impossible. A good coach will know all the strengths and weaknesses of his or her team (in whatever the team sport) and will devise the game plan accordingly.

In terms of your academic performance, you can think of all your skills, knowledge and abilities as being the 'team' you have to play with. You are empowered as the team coach to devise the 'game plan', and to make use of your 'players' as and when you will. You will have to make selections, order priorities, etc.

Exercise – List any skills, abilities or resources needed as the 'team coach' in your ambition to achieve a good standard in your studies. It is okay if you can only think of a few but those working in groups may be able to fill in all the spaces.

....

....

....

....

....

1.11 Address your weaknesses

Illustration – Further sports analogies

The encouragement to play to your strengths is not an exhortation to camouflage your weaknesses! If you play in a sports team, the opposition will quickly learn your weaknesses and will endeavour to exploit and capitalise on them. For example, if you were an attacking soccer or rugby player and could only kick with your right foot, the opposition would try to force you into a position where you could only kick with your left foot. The best long-term solution to this would be plenty of practice on your weak foot on the training ground until you feel it is strong

(Continued)

(Continued)

enough to use in a competitive match. A tennis player who has aspirations to win a grand slam (Wimbledon, US Open, French and Australian Opens) will not achieve this if he or she only has a very good forehand. Tennis players will only dramatically improve their world-ranking position when they have learned to use their backhand also (as well as other qualities such as good first serve, second serve, return serve, ability to volley, etc.).

If you can clearly identify your weaknesses from the exercises in the chapters that follow, then these are the issues that you should seek to improve, while not allowing the strengths you have already developed to lapse. An important aim of the book is to help you identify your personal strengths and weaknesses by exercises based on objective criteria, and to use this information for your personal development.

SUMMARY

Chapter 1 summary points

➢ Use familiar ground and previous strengths to build on

➢ Previous exam experience can serve you well again

➢ Use course work skills to benefit exam performance

➢ Exam experience will equip you with transferable and lasting skills

➢ Identify and address exam-related problems one by one

2 Learning Processes and Preferences

2.1 Adapt a positive exam perception

It is quite possible to underachieve at university and to remain in a static state of mediocrity in terms of your performance. Exams play an important role in your overall achievement, so how you think in relation to them, and to the learning process associated with them, is important. The aim of this chapter is to challenge your mindset about exams (if needed), and to guide you towards effective adjustment.

Exercise – Troubleshooting on exam problems

First, read over the following list and circle a number from 1 to 5 as appropriate, according to the code that follows (avoid 3 unless you have to use it):

1 = Strongly agree. 2 = Agree. 3 = In between. 4 = Disagree. 5 = Strongly disagree.

(Continued)

(Continued)

1.	I generally underachieve in my exams	1 2 3 4 5
2.	I have a good exam revision strategy	1 2 3 4 5
3.	Exams are not my strong point	1 2 3 4 5
4.	My time management in exams is very good	1 2 3 4 5
5.	I take too long choosing exam questions	1 2 3 4 5
6.	I feel very confident when I approach exams	1 2 3 4 5
7.	I rely chiefly on my course work to boost my grades	1 2 3 4 5
8.	I cope very well with exam stress	1 2 3 4 5
9.	My memory techniques are inadequate	1 2 3 4 5
10.	My technique for exam rough work is efficient	1 2 3 4 5
11.	I stick to my exam methods although I know they can be improved	1 2 3 4 5
12.	I use a good structure for my exam essays	1 2 3 4 5
13.	My exam grades are a poor reflection of the effort I invest	1 2 3 4 5
14.	My writing style is clear and easy to follow	1 2 3 4 5

You have a positive perception of your exam ability if you tended to answer towards 'agree' to the statements with even numbers (2, 4, 6, 8, 10, 12 and 14), and towards 'disagree' to the statements with odd numbers (1, 3, 5, 7, 9, 11 and 13). Don't worry if you think your score is disappointing – treat this information as useful knowledge that will help you get more out of the book. The issues will be worked out in more detail in this and subsequent chapters.

2.2   Making imaginative use of resources

Illustration – Style or fashion?

Fashion in dress is chosen and directed by the gurus in the fashion world and is then marketed in trendy magazines, by celebrities and through shows on the catwalk. It is then distributed by retail fashion outlets. The momentum is kept going by 'dedicated followers of fashion' who read the magazines, which are like a bible to the faithful. In order to conform to the changing trends in fashion, individuals do not have to be creative or original. Rather, all they have to do is keep up with the moving trends and ensure that they have a healthy bank balance! On the other hand, a stylish person may not follow every fashion that emerges on the High Street, but can still dress in a fresh, imaginative and appealing manner. Indeed, they may blend colours and styles in a way that complements and enhances their own physical features (contours, complexion, hair, eye colour, physique, etc.).

It may surprise some students to know that fashions and trends are also characteristic of the academic world. Government policies sometimes change the educational agenda and quality control bodies ensure that these are implemented. This does not mean that all the changes that come are a bad thing, but sometimes we end up going back to where we started before the experiment! At present, exams represent one of the issues in the melting pot, but many are arguing for their retention (alongside other methods of assessment).

One of the aims of this book is to help you with the learning and thinking styles that will serve you well irrespective of the changing vogues in assessment trends.

The following is a checklist of qualities that should be useful across a range of assessment methods.

Checklist – Timeless principles for learning and assessment

✓ Present a range of issues in a balanced format
✓ Include a critical approach to the treatment of a subject

✓ Show that arguments are underpinned by evidence
✓ Make good use of headings and subheadings (even as rough work)
✓ Do not pad out arguments with non-essential extras
✓ Keep a good clear structure and maintain a good flow of argument
✓ A problem-solving approach is a good strategy for argument
✓ Demonstrate both memory work and understanding
✓ Produce evidence that you have learned independently
✓ Integrate material from a range of sources and be up to date

Once you have identified the issues that will be beneficial to learning and assessment, you should also consider the issues that will detract from the quality of your learning, and these are highlighted below.

2.3   Never flog a dead horse

Most of us probably believe that, 'if it ain't broke, don't fix it!' On the other hand, it is foolish to persist stubbornly with a method that is clearly not working. In the words of a common adage, it is foolish to 'flog a dead horse'.

The lesson is to assess what will work and what will not, and to drop what will not work.

However, sometimes habits are so firmly entrenched that they are difficult to let go. Nevertheless, changes can be very liberating and can empower you with newfound confidence. It is important to give yourself some practice at different approaches to exams before attempting something novel in an exam situation. This is a more cautious approach in changing your exam strategies.

PRINCIPLES FOR CHANGING EXAM STRATEGY

- **Recognise the futility of methods that limit you**

- **Identify problem areas and earmark them for change**

- **Replace tired old ways with fresh new approaches**

- **Practise the changes in mock, self-chosen tests**

- Implement changes in a manageable manner

- Continue to monitor the need for change

EXAMPLES OF ISSUES THAT MAY NEED CHANGING

- Revision reading that is not focused and relevant

- Possessing too much loose material that is not organised

- Not reading exam questions carefully enough

- Leaving division of time and labour in exams to instinct rather than planning

- Too much monotony in learning activities

- Failure to 'export' and 'import' material across topics and subjects

- Heavy reliance on memory work alone

- Gambling on the 'right' questions coming up in an exam

- Tendency to present a lengthy descriptive introduction

- Complex and elaborate rough work that takes up too much time

- Resolution to return every detail presented in a lecture

- Determination to 'bend' the question into what was hoped for

Illustration – Two aspects of a recipe

Every individual has his or her own strengths and you should ensure that you capitalise on yours (although not at the expense of other aspects of your performance). For example, some individuals have an extraordinary memory but the danger is that they present their responses in a form that reads like a telephone directory! Take the example of a recipe. It is not sufficient to provide

(Continued)

(Continued)

a list of ingredients with all the exact measures needed. You must also present the method in which they are to be mixed in terms of order and strategy. Thus, if your strength is in understanding how the ingredients are mixed, it is also essential to remember to include the quantities for each substance. Applying this theory to exam techniques, the first step is to list the important names and facts (the ingredients) that have to be remembered. You can list these initially as part of your rough work. The second step is to relate 'the ingredients' to the question in the order and mix that is most suitable in addressing the issues raised in the question. So think of both ingredients and method as you approach your exams.

2.4   Thinking in style

According to Sternberg (1997), individuals are likely to differ in their preferred thinking styles and he identifies three major approaches. The first is the Executive style and this pinpoints the people who love to be creative. These are the people who enjoy the freedom of creating their own ideas and designing their own projects. The second is the Legislative style and this refers to the people who enjoy carrying out the plans and projects that others have designed. They have no desire to be original, and they enjoy making the plans of others work. The third category is the Judicial style and this describes the people who like to assess and to come up with constructive suggestions for improvement. At university, it would be an advantage to develop all three approaches, even if you feel you are strongest at one in particular. Some examples of how you might apply the three styles to learning activities or assessment tasks are presented below. (Codes: Executive = E, Legislative = L, Judicial = J).

- **Doing a multiple-choice exam (L)**

- **Reading over set material for revision (L)**

- **Planning out division of time and labour in an exam (E)**

- **Using efficient ways to remember material in mnemonics (E & L)**

- Writing a critical evaluation of evidence (J)

- Flexible ways to adapt what you have learned to the slant in a question (E)

Many of your academic tasks will require an integration of all styles although some tasks will be more oriented towards one.

2.5   Thinking in structure

It is claimed that we cannot cope with the bombardment of information that enters our minds on a daily basis unless we already have some established mental structures into which to fit the onslaught (Aronson et al., 1994). These are sometimes referred to as cognitive templates and their purpose is to help us make sense of the world and to prevent our minds from becoming chaotic. As you will later see, it will help your memory recall if you can learn your material in an organised manner. There is a range of useful memory techniques that you can profitably employ and some of these will involve a structured approach to learning. Think of how chaotic a public library would be if the books were not clustered under topics and arranged alphabetically by authors' names. Library staff cannot perform a good public service unless they ensure that their books are arranged carefully in order. In the same way you will profit from your learning if you pursue it in an organised way and you have an organised system for memory, note-taking, outlines, etc.

2.6   Thinking in substance

You cannot think adequately if you do not have the raw materials (i.e. basic information) to think with. As noted above, the method for the recipe is not enough without the list and quantities of the ingredients. If you write a critique in response to an exam, the quality of your work will be limited if you omit important aspects of the topic. You may not, for instance, know the most recent developments in research, and this may mean that your conclusions are out of date.

Illustration – Discovery of a new drug treatment

A student might cite that the cure for a certain disease had been found and that it was totally successful. He or she might be able to name the drug that has been used as the method of treatment and the researchers who had made the discovery and pioneered the tests. However, if there had been a number of recent reports concerning bad side-effects from the drug, and the student failed to mention these, then important information is missing. The result is an incomplete and inaccurate reflection of the effects of the drug. Therefore, in spite of the fact that the student may have been a critical thinker, the overall conclusion is somewhat inadequate.

In sum, you must ensure that you possess the range of relevant information to present an adequate critique.

TYPICAL COMMENTS MADE BY EXAMINERS ON EXAM SCRIPTS

Although the following comments are fictitious, they are not untypical of what examiners look for. They may give you some further insight into how you can continue to improve your exam strategy.

Deficient	Commendable
Lengthy introduction	Clearly and concisely written
Poor structure	Clearly structured presentation
Lacks evidence	Good use of evidence
Overly descriptive	Good quality critique
Loses focus	Maintains focus throughout

Lopsided arguments	Well balanced arguments
Limited content range	Wide content range
Weak in cited sources	Rich in cited sources
Question not directly addressed	Question adequately addressed

2.7 Thinking in sets

In 1942, A.S. Luchins carried out a series of experiments in which children had to solve a problem by pouring water into jugs of various shapes and sizes (Luchins, 1942, also cited in Hayes & Orrell, 1994). The children learned to work out the solution by following a set sequence of actions. Once a 'learning set' had been established, Luchins introduced another problem that could be solved by a more simple and direct route. However, because the learning set had become entrenched, the children followed their usual routine and were 'blinded' to the more direct solution.

The lesson to be learned is that you should not automatically adopt a fixed approach to problems without first thinking if there is a better way to accomplish the task.

Sometimes we persist with methods even when we know that they could be much improved. Consider the following two lists. One refers to a set approach to exams and the other to a flexible approach. These are not either/or approaches – they illustrate when a set approach is best (first list) and when a flexible approach is best (second list).

Where a 'closed' or 'set' approach to exams might be best:

- **Early identification of questions to be targeted**

- **Distribution of tasks by division of time**

- **Reproduction of brief, memorised structures as rough work**

- **Preferred topic areas to tackle**

- **Back-up plan if preferred topics do not come up**

Where an 'open' or 'flexible' approach is more likely to be fruitful:

- Exclude prepared material that is not relevant

- Re-arrange memorised outlines around the slant in the question

- Change the order of prepared points and omit irrelevant points

- Change the emphasis of prepared points (e.g. subheadings to main headings)

- 'Import' material from other topics (if it blends in smoothly)

2.8   Thinking in systems: to converge or diverge?

Illustration – A Greek philosopher and a bucket of water

A man threw a bucket of water over the philosopher Archelaus as an insult. When Archelaus failed to react, he was asked how he managed to remain calm in the face of provocation. His answer was that the person had not thrown the water over the true Archelaus, but over the man the attacker thought Archelaus was! Archelaus was able to look at the problem in a different way and see his attacker in a different light. He was convinced that the man would not have thrown the water if he had known the true nature of Archelaus. Perhaps if the philosopher had reacted angrily and retaliated he would have confirmed the attacker's negative perceptions. In short, Archelaus could see much more clearly than his attacker and was, by his calmness, in effect helping the aggressive person with his blindness.

The application of this story to an exam situation is don't just rush in with the first idea that pops into your head. Hold off for a moment or two while you jot down various possibilities. It may well be that a richer interpretation of the question will emerge as you engage your mind with various possibilities. This is further reinforced in the example of children's learning and development.

The Swiss psychologist Piaget identified stages of learning that children are likely to pass through in their cognitive development. He suggested that children go through a phase in which they are 'ego-centric', i.e. they see objects only from their own stand-point. One of Piaget's typical experiments was designed to demonstrate children's need to emerge from this limited stage of development. He would place a model mountain in the centre of a table with the child observing an object, such as a doll, at the side of the mountain visible to them. At the other side of the model mountain would be another object that the child could not see but that was visible to the experimenter at the other end of the table. When the child was asked what they saw, they were usually able to describe the object in front of them quite clearly. However, the crucial test was when they were asked to describe what the experimenter saw at the other side.

His experiments demonstrated that children were not always able to realise that what a person saw who was at the opposite end of a table to them was different from what they saw at their end of the table. At some stage in the children's development they learn, according to Piaget, to 'de-centre' and identify correctly the object that the person opposite sees rather than the object that they see. It can further be argued that same principle also operates in the social world. Social development and maturity come when we can project ourselves into other people's position and see things from their standpoint. An old proverb advises that we should never criticise another person until we have walked a mile or two in their shoes.

The principle can finally be extended to thinking and learning (and therefore to your approach to your assessments and exams). Instead of going into 'automatic pilot' about set ways to learn and approach assessment tasks, you might consider employing some of the following techniques (these points are illustrated with examples throughout the book).

STRATEGIES FOR EFFECTIVE APPROACHES TO THINKING AND LEARNING

- **Make connections between various aspects of your topic**

- **Fit each unit of learning into the overall context of your study programme**

- Share resources mutually with others

- Set tasks and goals for each other and check that they are accomplished

- Set questions for each other and meet with prepared answers

- Meet together as a group and design the structure and sequence of a subject and how you would assess it

- Set problems for yourselves and structure the course material around the solutions

- Think of illustrations and applications that will make the material live

2.9 Thinking the unthinkable!

In addition to thinking styles, educationalists have also suggested learning styles. Examples of these are the activist style, the reflective style, the theorist style and the pragmatic style. You can try out the following measure (adapted and modified from an existing measure) in order to identify your preferred learning style(s).

Exercise – Tick whether you agree or disagree with each of the following statements.

Statement	Agree	Disagree
1. I usually interpret problems as opportunities		
2. My preference for learning is for practical situations		
3. Problems present me with a challenge I enjoy solving		
4. I prefer to have time to ponder over what I have learned		

(Continued)

	Agree	Disagree

(Continued)

5. I am not content until I have heard all aspects of arguments

6. I like to learn by observing others

7. I do not like to try things out before mastering the concepts

8. Without clear thinking and understanding I will not dabble with the practicalities

9. I generally need to know that I am working under clear guidelines

10. I am quite content to try things out before I work them out

11. I like the opportunity to discover things myself in practice

12. I prefer to work on without advice until I feel that I am ready to request it

The following clusters of statements represent a tendency towards:

(1–3)   An activist style

(4–6)   A reflective style

(7–9)   A theorist style

(10–12)   A pragmatic style

If you examine where you placed your ticks (i.e. 'agree' or 'disagree'), you can work out what your preferred learning style is.

It may be optimal for you to bring all these together and use elements from them all, even if you have a preference for one or two. If you set your eyes on personal growth, then you will be prepared to experiment with different thinking styles and learning styles. In your approach to your learning, variety will keep freshness in your work and will stimulate your personal development, while you will always have your personal strengths and preferences to fall back on for insurance.

If you reflect a little, you will see that you can take the same content, substance and information as everyone else and put it across in a manner that is fresh, innovative and memorable.

2.10   Deeper form of learning

The goal of true education is deep learning (Biggs, 1999) and the opposite of this is shallow learning. Deep learning means that you make the best possible use of your resources in the most thoughtful manner.

THE CHARACTERISTICS OF SHALLOW LEARNING

- Primary interest and focus is in the grade obtained (summative)

- Mechanical reproduction of material (memory work)

- Little interest in quality feedback

- Minimal motivation for the subject

- Little effort to stretch beyond the minimum required reading

- Procrastination in application to reading and revision

- Study is seen as little more than a passport to a job

- Suffers the kind of exam anxiety that arises from inadequate preparation

- Often content with learning at a descriptive level

THE CHARACTERISTICS OF DEEP LEARNING

- Values learning for its own sake

- Finds momentum from personal motivation

- Is seen as a life-long process

- Interested in learning to learn

- Uses understanding as well as memory

- Sets units of learning within an overall context

- Focuses on how skills can be transferred across modules and over years

- Recognises the value of learning principles for employability

- Looks for formative and diagnostic feedback

- Targets independent learning to complement set exercises

- Enjoys the challenge of problem solving and critical thinking

Exercise – As you reflect on the lessons of this chapter, what can you highlight to improve the quality of your learning? Write your own checklist.

✓ ....

✓ ....

✓ ....

✓ ....

✓ ....

SUMMARY

Chapter 2 summary points

➢ In all assessments aim for balance, criticism, evidence and structure

➢ Aim to avoid padding, mere description and dated material

➢ Pursue independent and problem-based learning

➢ Hold on to what works and let go of what doesn't

➢ Vary learning activities and find the styles that work best for you

3 Motivation: The Dynamics for Achievement

3.1 Can't live with or without motivation — facing the dilemma

Illustration — The Great Reformers

What was it that led the great reformers to push legislation, such as the Reform Bill of 1832, through the English Parliament? It was because they saw gross injustices, felt the need for change and believed that they could make a difference if they set the wheels of change in motion. For example, Lord Shaftesbury was influential in the campaign that led to the Reform Bill — an Act of Parliament that required workers to be treated with more dignity and humanity than before. The spirit behind the Bill was that all people should be valued and respected from the cradle to the grave. Lord Shaftesbury could trace the origins of his reforming campaign to an incident in which he observed a pauper's funeral.

(Continued)

(Continued)

The dead pauper was enclosed in a cheap, fragile box that was pulled on a handcart by a few drunken men. They stumbled on a hill, the box fell off and the pauper's body rolled out. The drunk attendants roared in fits of laughter, but Shaftesbury was so incensed that he felt strongly motivated to initiate a campaign that would bring dignity to the lives of ordinary people. While others may have been unmoved at or merely tolerated such incidents, the parliamentary reformers were stirred to action and did not rest until their envisaged reforms were achieved.

THE DYNAMICS OF MOTIVATION

Motivation is:

- **The dynamics behind progress**

- **The starting point for change**

- **The means for setting clear goals before you**

- **The force that enables you to plot a path to your goal**

- **The energy that formulates short-term and long-term goals**

Motivation can be an uncomfortable fact of life, for the person driven by it has no room for complacency. When motivation is properly possessed, controlled and channelled, it becomes the dynamic catalyst for change and progress.

Motivation encapsulates a perception of the need for change, a belief that the change can be effected and a willingness to commit the resources needed for change.

Motivation leads to the prioritisation of activities that sometimes includes the setting aside of other important tasks that can wait for another occasion. There was an English cricketer from the nineteenth century, C.T. Studd, who gave up his considerable wealth and the sport he loved to serve as a missionary in China and Africa. At first he was inclined to keep back part of his fortune for himself. However, with his wife's encouragement, he eventually surrendered all he had in order to further the cause he passionately believed in.

Checklist — To check out the level and consistency of your motivation, you might periodically

- ✓ Rethink your priorities
- ✓ Restructure your timetable
- ✓ Review your strategies
- ✓ Renew your commitment
- ✓ Keep your study folder material updated

Motivation may involve the re-ordering of priorities and a practical commitment to a belief in the value of the goal you are aiming for. In academic courses, some students are well motivated from start to finish, some acquire increasing motivation as they progress in their study programme, and some students never seem to 'get off the ground' in terms of motivation. There are many ways in which you can motivate yourself to fulfil your potential in academia, but the required cocktail may differ from student to student. It is therefore essential to learn, by whatever means, what factors motivate you in order to avoid complacency and mediocrity.

Motivating factors may be negative (e.g. fear of failure) or positive (e.g. success is the gateway to a professional career), or may be extrinsic (e.g. a better salary) or intrinsic (e.g. the satisfaction of being qualified to give others professional help), or a combination of all these.

Think of your motivation as an animal that must be fed if it is to be sustained, and you can use thoughts like those just outlined to nourish it.

Exercise — Write your own list of the factors that will inspire and motivate you, and how you can maintain your motivation at a steady level:

- ✓ ....
- ✓ ....
- ✓ ....
- ✓ ....
- ✓ ....

3.2 The dynamic link between ability and achievement

Researchers have asked the question why students with great ability sometimes fall short of their potential, while students with apparently limited potential exceed expectations (Spielberger et al., 1983). The short and simple answer is that there is more to achievement than ability, and one of the key features is motivation (Prosser, 1995). It is evident that some basic ability is required for successful academic performance, but the fact that you have satisfied your college's or university's entrance requirements means you have this level of ability – it is a vote of confidence in you. However, when you enter an exam room to take a test, a good level of ability in itself will not be enough. In this chapter the focus is on motivation, but also important are confidence and anxiety reduction and control techniques. Moreover, there should also have been a semester-long history of extracting and integrating material from a range of sources, compiling extended and summary notes, and preparation for revision. Furthermore, you need to enter the exam room with an exam strategy that will allow you to capitalise on your study and organisational skills. In order to work and prepare for the day when you will be tested, you will need the trigger of motivation to get you on your way again and again.

A car engine is comprised of many complex parts that allow the driver to travel at speed over long distances and for long periods of time. Without the initial spark to start the engine, however, the car remains stationary – a useless piece of metal that serves no greater purpose than as an object of admiration.

3.3 Getting motivated – a necessity for human progress

As we have seen, motivation provided the trigger for parliamentary reformers such as Lord Shaftesbury. At a biological level, we are motivated to replenish our bodies with food, water and sleep as the need arises. Socially, we may be motivated to find company or a mate, or sometimes to be assertive. Animals are motivated to explore their environment, and to provide for and protect their young. Motivation is a driving force to preserve and extend life and the opposite of motivation is apathy. If you are a motivated student, you will aim for much more than the maintenance of the standard you have reached – you will want to add to your knowledge and skills all the time.

It is clear that motivation is a basic fact of life and without it there would be no survival, reproduction or progress.

Exercise — Pause for thought

If you have already entered university or college, you may have moved from home to live in or near your academic institution.
You will already have experienced changes in your life at a personal and a social level, and some of these changes may not have been anticipated.

Make a list of some of the changes you had anticipated:

....

Make a list of some of the changes you had not anticipated:

....

List the reasons why you think students drop out in their first year at college or university:

....

Are exams or tests likely to be a factor?

List the factors that could motivate you to remain within college or university:

....

3.4 Motivation and mobilisation — translating aspiration into action

Motivation is a word that is associated with action. If a person does not act or get beyond talking about action, we conclude that the person is not sufficiently motivated.

Motivation entails not only sketching plans at the drawing board, but also carrying them out in the workshop.

Motivation is more than wanting, liking, desiring, preferring or aspiring; it requires work, effort, action and energy. True motivation should be measured by the effort invested to achieve plans, i.e. meaningful, targeted activity rather than a large amount of aimless activity.

Illustration – Enticing cooking

Academic researchers refer to an 'operational definition' of a given construct such as motivation. A simple example of an operational definition is a recipe. In order to create the finished product, such as Spanish Omelette, Hungarian Goulash or Greek Moussaka, all ingredients need to be included in the stipulated quantities, and these should be mixed together in the correct order and with the correct procedure. An excellent chef is one who not only knows what the textbooks say about culinary skills, but who can also improvise to produce seductive smells, alluring presentations and enticing tastes. But he or she will need a framework to work within to allow for this kind of effective spontaneity.

If you are truly motivated to prepare for your exams, you will begin to plan for these as soon as possible.

Putting off tasks is the death knell for motivation, but even small actions can fan the flame of motivation.

You can initially feed your thoughts and preparations by asserting to others that you intend to engage in planned activities, but this in itself will not be sufficient to maintain momentum. If the chef begins by bringing together all the ingredients and sets out all the utensils that he needs (knife, scales, blender, jug etc.), this will provide the initial dynamic to consolidate his motivation. A little action to begin revision may prove to be more advantageous than meticulous plans that never materialise.

Exercise — Write your own checklist of the factors that may dampen your motivation in your academic life.

✓ ....

✓ ....

✓ ....

✓ ....

✓ ....

3.5 Mechanics and dynamics — aspects of human personality

Illustration — Optimism as motivation for achievement

A study summarised by Goud & Arkoff (2003) reports that the insurance company Met Life invited psychologist Martin Seligman to advise on recruiting salespeople. Up to that point Met Life had used a simple aptitude test. Seligman encouraged them to continue with this but also to use a test of optimism. He suggested that Met Life should not only employ all those who passed the aptitude test, but also those who failed the aptitude test but scored highly on dispositional optimism. The company followed this advice and monitored how these new employees fared in sales over the next couple of years. They found that the optimism group registered a 21 per cent higher rate of sales than the aptitude group after one year, and this differential rose to 57 per cent by the end of the second year. This example illustrates the point that there is more to being successful than ability. Goud and Arkoff concluded that the optimistic salespeople are less likely to be daunted or deterred by negative responses, refusals and bad times when sales figures are low. They will persevere in the belief that fortunes will improve through time if effort remains consistent.

It is evident that true motivation is not merely associated with an initial flush of enthusiasm, but manifests itself in resilience of spirit. In television wildlife programmes showing lions hunting, there may be a number of unsuccessful chases before the lion eventually succeeds. Sometimes the lions are exhausted by the failed attempts. They may have to conserve energy and employ less extravagant hunting strategies. But it is essential that they do not lose their motivation to stay alive, to secure their prey and to feed themselves and their young. Motivation is sustained by the belief that the end result will be achieved even after initially unsuccessful 'sorties'.

Exercise — Now write your own checklist of the opportunities (that come and go) that you must seize at university:

✓ ....

✓ ....

✓ ....

✓ ....

✓ ....

3.6 When motivation is misguided

Aristotle used to assert that virtue is defined as the mean between two extremes. For example, he would have argued that extreme forms of anger are dangerous, reckless and counterproductive. Conversely, a lack of anger may suggest someone has little passion or emotion, and such a person may be living a lacklustre life. True anger would be for the right reason, at the right level of intensity and for the proper duration. The strength of this emotion could then be used to correct an injustice or redress an imbalance. On the one hand, the person lacking emotion has suppressed an important element of what it means to be human and, on the other hand, the person with excessive, uncontrolled emotion has lost sight of the adaptive purpose (i.e. making the adjustments you need to fit into and survive in a new or changing environment) that emotions can serve when measured and deployed properly.

In academia you can be motivated to excel in your studies, but this should not be at the expense of other qualities that should also be cultivated. For example, if you are to function effectively in the social world, you will need social skills such as good communication and interpersonal skills. Being motivated does not mean that you cannot enjoy leisure activities and times of relaxation both alone and with others. Without rest and breaks, our minds will not function as effectively as they should do. 'All work and no play make Jack a dull boy'. Furthermore, motivation does not mean that you need to block the pathway of others in order to get to the top. In the western world the educational system has been designed to be competitive. There need not be anything wrong with that if everyone has the same opportunities.

Perhaps the best approach of all is to compete against the standards you set for yourself.

Motivation should not be the dynamic that leads us to sacrifice cultivating the many good social qualities that will prepare us to function effectively in the world of work.

Checklist – Some features that reveal the unhealthy excesses of motivation

✓ When you do not allow yourself outlets for fun and relaxation
✓ When you feel guilty every time you stop for a break
✓ When you keep working beyond the point where your mind feels saturated
✓ When you are severely disrupting your regular patterns of sleeping and eating
✓ When you aim for immediate goals that will take longer to achieve

3.7 Sub-goals as the pathways to the main goal

The primary focus of this book is on performance in an exam or test situation, but it is stressed that exam performance cannot be isolated from the rest of the academic programme. You do not become a completely different person when you walk into an exam room for you bring with you all the rich experience and knowledge that you have accumulated in your academic and personal life. All the little goals that you have set yourself over the semester have brought you to the threshold of your immediate goal of achieving a good standard in your exam.

Every time you have gone to a lecture, a seminar, a tutorial or every time you went to the library, opened a textbook, conducted a computer search or made some revision notes, you have edged your way towards better preparation for your exams.

Moreover, each test has armed you with more knowledge and experience for the next one. A primary goal should be to achieve a good level of consistency across all your assignments and assessments so that you will end up with a degree that will reflect the efforts you have invested and the qualities you have acquired.

Illustration — Learning to play the guitar

Individuals learn to play the guitar for a variety of reasons. It is likely that if you commit yourself to learning the guitar you will have more than one reason. Some reasons may be that you love to make music and you admire those who can produce creative sounds. You may like the thought of bringing enjoyment to others and perhaps you also feel that it will make you more cool, attractive, admired or respected. Maybe you want to meet others who have a similar taste in music. If you sit down and work out the 'cost' of learning to play the guitar, you may come to the conclusion that the end result is well worth it.

Motivation means that you will value the goals you are working towards and will invest the time, effort, patience and money that it takes to get you there. You may have to do some of the following on your journey to attain your goal of playing the guitar:

- Finding the money to pay for lessons (perhaps sacrificing other things)

- Finding the money to buy a guitar of your choice

- Investing the hours in practice (at the expense of other things)

- Finding courage to perform in front of others

- Being determined to persist when progress is slow and mastering tasks seems impossible

- Being willing to go over the basics again and again even when this is monotonous

- Working patiently towards producing a new song even when it seems far away

- Never losing sight of the end goal and the bigger picture

A glance at the above list will show you that motivation is a quality that will carry you through slow times, hard times, uncertain times and frustrating times.

3.8   The hidden cost of reward in extrinsic sources of motivation

The Hidden Costs of Reward is the title of a book by Lepper and Greene (1978), which suggests that play can be turned into work if the primary motive becomes the external reward. For example, an individual may become a professional sportsperson because of his or her love for a sport, but as fame, media attention, celebrity status and financial rewards encroach, these may become the primary goals in the individual's life. A famous slogan says 'Power corrupts; absolute power, corrupts absolutely'. Politicians may initially aspire to office to serve the needs of the people they were elected to represent, but a craving to maintain a position of power may, through time, displace these commendable goals. Whole political parties may engage in all manner of political point-scoring, posturing and cosmetic activities in an attempt to ensure re-election. An old theologian is reported to have said that most people can cope with failure fairly well but that few are equipped to handle success (as it may chip away at our good qualities).

Perhaps for many students their problem is the other way round – their real need is to turn their work into play! It may well be that many students come to college or university with extrinsic sources of reward as their primary motivating goals – they want a good degree classification, leading to a professional career and a good income to follow that! Elliot and Dweck (1988) found that children who used performance goals (i.e. their primary aim was to achieve good results to please teachers and parents and to compare favourably with peers) did not perform as efficiently and effectively as children who had learning goals.

The children who had learning goals had a style that facilitated mastery of the material and they aimed to improve their competence, but the children with performance goals had a helpless style and aimed to establish their ability and to avoid feeling inadequate. It is said that in the ancient school of Athens, students saw themselves as scholars in their subject in their first year, and saw themselves as wise in their subject in their second year. Finally, as they advanced in their studies, they saw themselves as students and learners. They realised, in an often-cited old analogy, that they were just picking up a pebble of information here and there on the beach, but before them lay the whole ocean of truth.

The meaning of the word 'philosopher' is 'lover of wisdom' and therefore lover of true learning. True philosophers have more questions than answers – their love of learning for its own sake is the motivation that guarantees quality learning. George Bernard Shaw once said that the true artist would rather let his family beg, starve and go bare foot than sell his books. Perhaps this was intended to be a metaphorical way of advocating the maintenance of learning for its own sake, rather than the pursuit of external rewards associated with it. Ironically, if you can fall in love with your subject and focus your motivation on learning, you may be more likely to achieve the rewards associated with success.

Exercise – Tick any of the following 14 points if you think it is likely to motivate you towards increased application to your university course.

Salary	Self-respect	Expectations of others ......
Career	Usefulness to others	Fear of failure ......
Security	Love for subject	Status with degree ......
Knowledge	Challenge of learning	Attract partner ......
Understanding	Unpleasant alternatives	

Goals that are internal include the challenge of learning, gaining understanding, love for the subject, and usefulness. According to the theory outlined above, these internal motives are more likely to bring out our best efforts. The other motives are driven by factors such as money, power, status and fear. If we can develop an enjoyment for our chosen subject, and a commitment to it irrespective of the rewards that may come from studying it, we are more likely to learn it at a deeper level.

3.9   Lessons from Self-Determination Theory

Self-Determination Theory was proposed by Ryan and Deci (2000). The essence of the theory is that people perform optimally, and have a greater sense of personal well-being, if they are not primarily driven by the expectations and evaluations of others. In their research, Ryan and Deci found that the primary needs of individuals are Competence, Autonomy and Relatedness (CAR). When individuals are driven by the expectations and evaluations of others, this is associated with anxiety, fear and guilt and how to reduce these. However, when individuals are motivated by a greater sense of personal well-being, this is associated with personal growth and development. This is consistent with the emphasis of Carl Rogers and Abraham Maslow, who were committed to the belief that people in general have enormous potential for personal growth, given the right conditions and encouragement. They did not stop at the reduction or elimination of anxiety and fear, but pointed to the pathway for progress and achievement. Therefore their keynotes of confidence, self-worth and goal achievement point to a positive approach to challenging tasks such as exams.

3.10   The 'flow experience' – a higher form of learning

The 'flow experience', proposed by Csikszentmihalyi (1975), describes the experience in which you are so engrossed in what you are doing that you almost lose track of time, environment and consequences.

During exams it is essential to keep a close eye on time, but this restriction is not always necessary during the learning experience.

You may, for example, think of reading an enjoyable novel, such as *Lord of the Rings*. You may be so curious that you 'burn the midnight oil' in order to progress deeper into the plot. Many commentators have commended J.K. Rowling for her series of Harry Potter books because she has, in effect, assisted children in getting into the flow experience of reading. Young children have waded their way through the large texts because the characters have intrigued them and the plots have fascinated them.

The same applies to work activities and some people regard job satisfaction as a top priority. If you enjoy your job, it will seem as though time flies when you are at work, but work may not seem so palatable in a highly stressed environment. For example, health service workers may derive great personal satisfaction from helping others, but may also feel that enjoyment is impaired by the relentless bombardment of patients or clients who need their help.

> *When planning is poor and revision is put off, pressure mounts and enjoyment is minimised or removed.*

Students will sometimes inform lecturers or tutors that they know which staff members really enjoy the subjects they teach, and they will observe that this comes across in the teaching sessions. Similarly, educators should be able to tell if the students they teach are enjoying the learning experience. Some good advice once given to teachers was that if they do not strike oil after a given time, they should stop boring!

> *Enjoyment can also be communicated through writing and it is often clear to an examiner that a student has taken pride and joy in doing his or her work.*

It should be your aim as a student to enjoy your learning experience as much as possible and communicate this in your tests and exams. If there is enthusiasm and motivation for the subject matter, the learning will be more pleasurable and the tests will be less daunting.

3.11   Apparent failure — a trigger for motivation

Illustration — A lesson from two eminent female writers

One of the most popular fiction writers in the UK was Catherine Cookson. When she sent her first book to the publishers, she was more or less told that writing

(Continued)

(Continued)

was clearly not her vocation and she was, frankly, wasting her time trying to pursue it. The person who made that early judgement did not have the insight or foresight to see the potential that would later unfold. More recently, J.K. Rowling had a similar problem as a number of reputable publishers were not interested in her work. Eventually Bloomsbury decided that the proposed Harry Potter series was worth the risk, and that positive decision paid dividends for the publishers and the author herself. What these two writers shared was that they never lost faith in themselves or their work, even when recognised authorities did not share their beliefs. The value of their work is now recognised by millions and both have confounded the early critics. Each knew that they could tell an enthralling story at a simple, one-to-one level, but it required determination and persistence to project this talent on to a much larger stage. The experience of these gifted women could be told over and over again, not only in literature but also in sport, the theatre, music, politics, the media, etc.

It is unquestionably true that negative evaluations from authority figures can undermine confidence, destroy morale and impair motivation. In some cases it has taken students years to recover from careless and disparaging remarks made by teachers. One woman reported that she was afraid to develop computer skills because one teacher described her as a 'stupid woman' simply because she had forgotten her password. Later she attained high academic status and found employment in a professional position. However, she believed the 'lie' she had been told, until she was eventually motivated to prove it wrong.

You do not have to own the negative evaluation that someone else has pronounced upon you.

3.12   Why the best teams don't always win

A sports team full of star performers, and hotly tipped to win, may lose because:

- **It has not gelled together as a team**

- **Individual team members are over-confident and complacent**

- They underestimate the opposition and take victory for granted

- They do not want the success badly enough

- They do not properly value the fans who support them

- They do not have sufficient pride in their club

There is much truth in the maxim that 'a faint heart never won a fair lady', for the fair lady may make her final decision based on who it is that wants her most. Motivation is such a crucial factor in any performance, and you can be very highly motivated to do the simplest task if you value the task or some important outcome associated with it.

People who are motivated will value the outcome they are striving to achieve. They will not be thrown off course when obstacles are set in their way, and they may even achieve more than others predicted and expected of them.

Years ago when a clergyman was being ordained, he was given this modicum of advice:

- Keep in touch with God

- Keep in touch with people

- Bring God and people together

His whole future ministry was summarised in those three simple imperatives and these were to shape and direct his motivation. For the student in the academic world, the message is:

- Keep in touch with the direction given for your assignments

- Keep up to speed with your personal study targets

- Bring the two elements together continually to keep on course for success

Capable students who are not motivated will fall short of their potential; average students who are motivated will confound their strongest critics. Some authors have been singled out for criticism because they have not fulfilled their potential in terms of the works they have produced. What they have left us is very good, but there is so much more that they could have written but did not. The extent of their influence is therefore limited.

Exercise — As a final exercise, summarise the major factors that you can use to measure and maintain your academic motivation (some may be repeats from previous exercises).

Academic motivation

| 1 | 2 | 3 | 4 | 5 | 6 | 7 |

1. ....

2. ....

3. ....

4. ....

5. ....

6. ....

7. ....

SUMMARY

Chapter 3 summary points

> ➤ Motivation provides the vision and dynamics for positive change

> ➤ Motivation enables you to make best use of your qualities and skills

> ➤ The true measure of motivation is consistent action

> ➤ Motivation functions within the framework of good planning

> ➤ Strong motivation will prevent you from being thrown off course

4 Confidence Building Measures

OBJECTIVES

This chapter will:

➤ Encourage you to set achievable goals
➤ Challenge you to maintain momentum in routine tasks
➤ Inspire you to monitor and review your progress
➤ Encourage you to change beliefs that hinder progress
➤ Guide you to develop confidence that works

4.1 Don't just talk about walking

This piece of advice implies that you should not just express good intentions but should translate those intentions into action. It has been suggested that when all is said and done, there is always more said than done! Soldiers are not trained to remain in a barracks but to go out where the heart of the action is. The only way to fulfil the purpose that one has been trained for is to engage in the activity prepared for, whether this relates to sports, education, industry, etc.

Talking has a valuable place in the scheme of things but is not an end in itself. In one case it was proposed that a group of politicians should get together for some preliminary verbal exchanges about the strategy and substance of their later fully-fledged discussions. A wit later referred to these preliminary sessions as 'talks about talks'! Sceptical observers of the talks about talks came to the conclusion that the whole exercise was a talking stunt designed to go nowhere.

In ancient Hebrew, a 'word' meant an active agent that left the speaker's mouth and went out to accomplish an action. It was important that a word should not 'fall to the ground'. A word was a active agent that accomplished an important mission, and we all know that words can encourage, inspire, help, heal, diffuse tension or hurt, harm, humiliate, divide and inflame. One of the weakest uses of words is when we promise ourselves that we will do something but do not carry out our stated intentions. If there is no one to hold us to our promise, we may be rather lacklustre in the discharge of our duty. It is possible to fall short of our verbalised intentions so often that we lose confidence in our own ability to accomplish much with our lives.

Promise yourself less, carry it out more often and your confidence will grow.

Exercise – Make a short checklist of exam-related tasks that really are achievable for you in preparation for your next batch of exams.

✓ ....

✓ ....

✓ ....

✓ ....

✓ ....

4.2 Setting achievable goals

We previously noted that it is possible to lose confidence in ourselves by promising more than we are able to deliver, or by being like the pelican, whose beak, according to the old rhyme, can hold more that its belly can!

The setting of unrealistic goals can become so daunting that you may leave yourself feeling immobilised.

However, it is sometimes the case that confidence can be undermined because other people have put us down and have shown no faith in us, to the extent that we lose much of our self-belief. A tradesman continually referred to his apprentice, endeavouring to learn his trade, as an old comic character, 'Useless Eustace!' Although this was quite witty to a squad of men on a building site, it was not a great source of inspiration to the young man who had to overcome the negative jibes. Similar anecdotal stories have been told of pupils and students in education. Some teachers used to think they had a divine right to pronounce decrees against pupils if they thought they had no academic or intellectual potential. Thankfully there has been a seismic shift toward improving the atmosphere of education. Educators now advocate that there should not only be a clear context in which to learn, but also a good atmosphere to facilitate learning (e.g. Gibbs, 1992; Ramsden, 1992). A good atmosphere entails the reduction of anxiety and the climate in which confidence can grow.

The starting point for developing confidence might not only be overcoming your past downfalls, but also surmounting the memories of previous taunts from educators or peers who could not see your latent potential.

Checklist — Setting achievable goals for exams

✓ Improve your average mark across exams
✓ Keep to self-imposed time limits for each question
✓ Cite more studies more succinctly
✓ Prepare clear structures for tackling exam questions
✓ Have well-organised revision notes (in both extended and condensed forms)
✓ Start your revision in good time
✓ Read questions carefully before tackling them
✓ Ensure you spend equal time revising the range of exam topics
✓ Find a good balance between revision and relaxation
✓ Enter the exam room with a sense of confidence and control

4.3 Moving forward in steady incremental steps

Illustration — 'Pacabel's Canon'

'Pacabel's Canon' is a piece of classical music that has been made popular in recent years by buskers on the street. There is something enchanting about the music and the explanation for this is found partly in the way the composer constructed it. Two bass notes are played at the same pace all the way through, but the speed of the melody gradually increases from start to finish. The overall effect of the steady time of the two bass notes, and the increasing speed of the melody, combine to produce a magical, musical effect. If you were to listen to the steady, unvaried plod of the two bass notes alone, the effect would be monotonous and unappealing. Nevertheless, the steady beat provides the necessary background on which the piece of musical genius has been built.

The application of this illustration is that some aspects of academic life appear to be routine and monotonous, such as attending lectures, seminars and tutorials; taking notes from books, journals and computer searches; preparing outline drafts for assignments, tests and exams; reading through set chapters from books and 'filling in the blanks' after a lecture. All the time this is going on, however, something is growing steadily in the background. You are developing qualities that include the ability to focus, integrate, analyse and produce quality critique. In addition, you are learning how to discriminate, summarise and economise in the use of your time and academic material. What is going on in the background with reference to the larger picture is that you are developing skills that will prepare you not only to tackle academic tasks effectively, but also to function efficiently in your career beyond graduation.

Exercise — Make a short checklist of some of the key skills you are developing that will serve you well both before and beyond graduation.

(Continued)

(Continued)

✓ ....

✓ ....

✓ ....

✓ ....

✓ ....

Some of the things you may have thought of for the above exercise might include: an ability to communicate effectively in writing and speech; an ability to gather information from a range of sources; the capacity to look at all sides of an argument objectively; skill in the use of computers; confidence in facing testing situations; working both in teams and independently; and working with focus under time pressure.

4.4   Monitoring your progress

A frustration for some students may come from a failure to notice any apparent progress in their work. Even when marks improve, not all students are convinced that this is attributed to personal academic growth. In one sense this is understandable because in physical growth we do not see ourselves develop overnight. The world would be a much less predictable place if people could grow one foot taller overnight! Over longer periods of time, however, we can observe gradual progress in height and from time to time we can confirm this by checking our progress in inches or centimetres. Similarly, your growth in academic work may be so slow that it is not noticeable over short spans of time. But if you are steady and persistent in your application to your work, you will doubtless learn principles and processes that will facilitate your academic development.

When you have learned the solid principles that will help you steer your way ahead clearly, it is important to keep the faith with these even in bad days when marks may plummet.

Exercise — Personal confidence

Look back at some of your previous work and note the improvements you have made. Some examples may be:

- Observe how the structure of your work has improved

- Note how the style of your sentences is clearer

- Underline how you have responded positively to feedback received

- Observe how you rely more strongly on cited evidence

- Notice that your arguments are more balanced than before

- Highlight how you cut to the chase more efficiently in preparation

- Take account of the fact that you would now submit a better assignment

There is no point looking back to past failures and then concluding that that is the way you will always be. Each student should look forward to personal progress and development in their academic work. It is good to look back in order to learn from past mistakes, but not to hinder your progress by feeling that you will just go on repeating your mistakes.

One mature student came and asked if he was 'playing in the right ball park'. He feared that he did not have the repertoire of skills that would enable him to obtain a good degree. His tutor was able to assure him that, although there was room for continued growth and improvement, the student had clearly demonstrated his skills and would achieve a good standard if he continued to apply himself in the way that he had done.

Exercise — Monitor your growth across your study programme

Although there are some skills that are unique to exams, such as working within strict time limits, exam skills are not totally independent of

(Continued)

(Continued)

other academic skills. Your growth in your general academic abilities will feed directly into your exam or test skills. In order to encourage your confidence in your overall growth (and to identify where you can improve) try to rate yourself on the following scale in terms of your academic development on each item. Circle the number that most accurately describes you, according to the following code:

1 = Lapsed noticeably. 2 = Lapsed slightly. 3 = Remained static. 4 = Marginal progress. 5 = Marked progress.

1.	Profiting from the lectures I attend	1	2	3	4	5
2.	Economy in reading	1	2	3	4	5
3.	Efficiency in note-taking	1	2	3	4	5
4.	Organisation in revision	1	2	3	4	5
5.	Consolidation after initial learning	1	2	3	4	5
6.	Use of library facilities	1	2	3	4	5
7.	Use of computers	1	2	3	4	5
8.	Sketching outline plans	1	2	3	4	5
9.	Developing transferable skills	1	2	3	4	5
10.	Contribution to small groups	1	2	3	4	5
11.	Control of anxiety	1	2	3	4	5
12.	Time management	1	2	3	4	5
13.	Writing critically	1	2	3	4	5
14.	Maintaining task consistency	1	2	3	4	5

4.5 Working within a realistic personal framework

Although it is true that if you aim at nothing you will certainly hit it, it is also true that if you are overly optimistic in your short-term or long-term goals you may impede your progress towards them.

> *Be optimistic by all means, but not through misty optics!*

For some students the problem is getting motivated to maintain a consistent level of work. If that is your primary problem, then consult Chapter 3 on motivation. If your problem is channelling your high levels of motivation to get the most benefit, then that chapter is also applicable. At present, the focus is on the issue of confidence and this can only thrive when it is developed within a personal framework that is realistic. A politician may not be ready to be the Prime Minister until he or she has had some experience working in government departments such as the Treasury, Education, Health, the Home Office and the Foreign Office, etc. Therefore build your confidence from within your present position rather than trying to project yourself into some envisaged future position that is remote.

> *To grow in confidence and prepare yourself for your future roles you must start now by grasping the things that are within your immediate grasp. As the proverb says, 'A bird in the hand is worth two in the bush'.*

You can begin to experience more quality in your learning activities and learning experience by applying simple principles such as those described in Chapter 6 on memory. For example, you can learn more efficiently by processing material through a range of modes, such as:

- **Listening carefully in lectures and discussions**

- **Contributing verbally in small group discussions**

- **Note-taking in lectures and personal study**

- **Reading selectively from books, journals and the Internet**

You can also enhance your quality of learning by:

- Asking questions (spoken and written)

- Making connections between points

- Consolidating what you have learned by re-reading

- Stretching your learning capacity in modest but regular increments

The title of a famous pop song says that 'It started with a kiss' – a simple step that led to deeper friendship! Once you begin to work you will:

- Pick up momentum

- Feed motivation

- Increase in confidence

- Develop a taste for more

4.6   Changing personal belief systems

Entrenched belief systems are the most difficult thing in the world to change and people will often hold to them tenaciously long after they are past 'sell by' and 'use by' dates! Yet, strong beliefs, even if they are sincerely held, may not be true. Think about these points for a moment and see how problematic it may be if you convince yourself that you cannot progress beyond your current level of achievement (especially if this is low).

4.7   What do you believe?

Bandura's (1986, 1997) concept of self-efficacy (described below) was designed to help clients overcome intractable belief systems associated with the kinds of anxiety, fear or lack of confidence that impede or paralyse progress.

Before reading on you can attempt the following self-report exercise. You are encouraged to be as honest and accurate as you can as there are no right and wrong answers. Also try to avoid the middle neutral option unless you have to use it.

Exercise – Academic self-efficacy scale (McIlroy et al., 2000)

Circle the number below that most accurate describes your response to each statement, according to the following code:

1 = Strongly disagree. 2 = Disagree. 3 = Neutral. 4 = Agree. 5 = Strongly agree.

1. I am confident that I can achieve good exam results if I really put my mind to it.   1 2 3 4 5

2. If I don't understand an academic problem, I persevere until I do.   1 2 3 4 5

3. When I hear of others who have failed their exams, this makes me all the more determined to succeed.   1 2 3 4 5

4. I am confident that I will be adequately prepared for the exams by the time they come around.   1 2 3 4 5

5. I tend to put off trying to master difficult academic problems whenever they arise.   1 2 3 4 5

6. No matter how hard I try, I can't seem to come to terms with many of the issues in my academic curriculum.   1 2 3 4 5

7. I am convinced that I will eventually master those items on my academic course which I do not currently understand.   1 2 3 4 5

8. I expect to give a good account of myself in my end-of-semester exams.   1 2 3 4 5

9. I fear that I may do poorly in my end-of-semester exams   1 2 3 4 5

10. I have no serious doubts about my own ability to perform successfully in my exams.   1 2 3 4 5

This exercise was designed to consider your self-efficacy beliefs, a concept with which you may not be familiar but at which we will look in some detail in the sections that follow. In order to find your score on the above scale, take the following steps:

1. Reverse score items 1–4, 7, 8 and 10 (i.e. 1 = 5, 2 = 4, 3 = 3, 4 = 2, 5 = 1).

2. Add all your scores on each item to obtain a total score.

3. Compare this in relation to the midpoint of the scale (30) – higher than this is a positive score and lower is negative. Close to the midpoint is a marginal positive or negative, but the further away your score is, the more likely it is to reflect high or low self-efficacy beliefs.

4. Also examine your score on each item, as a high or low score will reflect positive or negative self-efficacy beliefs at a given point. The midpoint for each item is 3 but remember that some items should be reversed (see point 1 above).

4.8   The three aspects of self-efficacy

Self-efficacy has become a construct that is used in a whole range of applied domains such as education, sport, computing, career and health. Positive self-efficacy beliefs have been clearly associated again and again with better performance in all these spheres and many more. Moreover, it has been demonstrated that when self-efficacy beliefs improve, performance improves with them (Bandura, 1997). In its simplest form, self-efficacy is defined as an individual's belief in his or her own ability to perform a given task successfully. When this is put into practice, it emerges in three aspects – initiative in taking action, effort expended or invested in the action and persistence in the face of obstacles. Therefore, self-efficacy provides an excellent focal point in addressing the issue of confidence. Gecas (1989), however, stressed that self-efficacy beliefs must be pitched at approximately the right level, as under-confidence will demotivate and over-confidence will demoralise.

> *If you set a series of small tasks for yourself you can tick them off one by one as you achieve them. Your confidence will gradually build and you will be ready to stretch yourself for greater achievements.*

No athlete would go out to run the 26-mile marathon at the first attempt. There is a process of training and stretching the targets gradually before that high standard can be attained.

The first prong of self-efficacy (initiative) can simply be defined by what is sometimes observed on a branded t-shirt – 'just do it!' In other words, don't hesitate and put off the action. A person who always procrastinates will never develop strong self-efficacy beliefs. Self-efficacy is defined by function – it represents the difference between dipping your toes in the water and jumping in. Or, changing the metaphor, it is operational at the point where you decide to walk out into the arena and take the bull by the horns. In relation to your academic tasks, the point of your focus should not be on doubts, fears or excuses, but on engaging with the immediate challenge.

The second facet of self-efficacy is effort, and this implies investment of time and this in turn suggests that the individual values the goal they are labouring to achieve. In the chapter on motivation, we considered both external and internal factors that can be valued in your academic career. You may want to pause for a moment to complete the next exercise.

Exercise – Make a list of the things you are willing to sacrifice (or suspend) in order to achieve your academic goals.

- ....

- ....

- ....

- ....

- ....

Self-efficacy also embodies motivation, again demonstrating that self-efficacy is a practical concept. It is essential that the architect sits and draws up plans for the building to be constructed, but these plans will amount to nothing unless the building contractor has the confidence to take the plans and begin to dig foundations, lay brick, etc.

The third aspect of self-efficacy is persistence, and this means that you will persist at a task when problems, obstacles and setbacks encroach. It is therefore clear that self-efficacy in its final form refers to the completion of a given task and the three aspects highlighted point to the practical demonstration of confident personal beliefs.

> *You start by taking the initiative through engaging with the task. You continue by investing the effort and commitment required to continue with the task. You persist to the end when you encounter problems that appear to be designed to deflect you from your chosen pathway.*

Perhaps you can make a list of some of the issues that you have stalled on in your course of study? This might help you to focus, pick the ball up, run with it and carry it over the line.

Exercise – Make a list of the issues that you could target for improvement, e.g. issues that you may have stalled on in the past and that have hindered your progress.

- ....

- ....

- ....

- ....

- ....

4.9   Additional features of self-efficacy

Bandura (1997) demonstrated experimentally that as self-efficacy beliefs improve, performance improves commensurately. These findings are inspiring to confidence in a couple of important ways:

- No one should feel locked into or trapped at their current level of performance

- Recent evidence of improvement should encourage the pursuit of further development

Bandura (1986) also argues that the development of self-efficacy stems from four sources:

1. Linkages to the emotions and the autonomic nervous system which is an aspect of the nervous system that is triggered when we become aware of danger or a demanding challenge. Symptoms of its activity include nervousness, trembling, sweating, breathlessness, etc. It is designed to put us into a state of alertness and preparedness. It will be fully addressed in Chapter 5 on anxiety, but suffice to say here that control of fear and nerves helps to clear the path to progress.

2. Verbal persuasion or the verbal encouragement of others (e.g. a tutor or parent). A well-timed, well-aimed word of encouragement can provide the boost to confidence that an individual may need. For example, at a graduation dinner, the mother of a French student said to her: 'If you choose to go now and do a doctorate, I will support you. I believe in you and I know that you can accomplish this goal.' That was a powerful and genuine message of encouragement to proceed and develop.

3. Reference to past successes (Bandura concluded that this is the most important). It is invariably a good strategy to remember what you have achieved and to process your past successes. It is always wise to take note of the distance you have travelled so far, and to use your achievements to inspire further progress. Sometimes there is a 'tug-of-war' in our minds about whether we are capable of accomplishing certain tasks. One of the 'players' we need in our team to pull the rope in our direction is the ability to process our past successes in academia.

4. Reference to suitable models for inspiration. An ideal model is believed to be the one that is as comparable to the observer as possible (e.g. in age, gender, background and education). However, you may need to think of students who are a little further on in a study programme but who were at a similar level of achievement to you at your present stage. At one university students from the second and fourth years met at a scheduled session to chat about a placement in the third year. This was very beneficial for the second-year students, and the fourth-year students recalled how useful this had been for them two years previously.

Although the kind of meeting noted in point 4 above may not be formally organised at your university or college, it is wise to try to meet those more advanced in your course. They will know the pitfalls and hurdles and are well placed both to understand your doubts, fears, anxieties and uncertainties and to provide advice on how to progress steadily and smoothly through the programme.

It may be helpful for you to plot out your progress over your degree programme. This should both encourage you to continue what you are doing well and help you to identify some targets for improvement. A hypothetical example is provided in Figure 4.1.

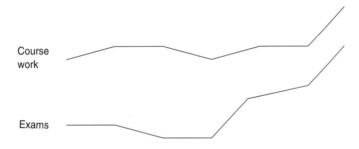

Course work marks start at 62% and end at 68%.
Exam marks start at 52% and end at 62%.

Figure 4.1   DIAGNOSTIC TEST OF MARKS – IDENTIFICATION OF TRENDS IN
PERFORMANCE OVER SEVEN POINTS IN TIME FOR COURSE WORK AND
EXAMS. THE UPWARD TRENDS REPRESENT IMPROVEMENTS IN ACHIEVEMENT

Several observations can be made about the performance trends of the fictitious example in Figure 4.1. For example:

- **The student is better at course work than exams**

- **In both tasks the student has generally been improving**

- **The downward dip in exams between points 2 and 4 might be explained by attention being diverted to course work**

- **This could be corrected by more balance planning of learning activities**

- **Most improvement has been in exams from the fourth point onwards**

If you cannot find the time to plot out a graph of your own academic performance, you can at least maintain a mental picture of your performance to date. If you have this information, you can chat to your personal tutor about the aspects of your study programme that you really need to target for improvement.

4.10 Achievement breeds on and feeds off confidence

It should first be noted that the definition of success can be relative, personal and subjective. A successful season for one sports team might be to avoid relegation or make a marginal improvement on their position from the previous year. Another team might conclude that finishing outside the top three in the league is disastrous, and for some nothing but top position will suffice! It is just the same in academia.

> *You may judge your standards of success with your peers, or with your own previous standards or against the future goals you have set yourself.*

You should make your own decision about how you want to define success and some students might prefer to set a standard slightly above their current level of achievement in order to ensure that they will stretch themselves just a little more at each hurdle.

> *Ensure that you design a goal strategy that can boost your confidence and keep your motivation intact.*

For example, you could opt to 'up the stakes' a little each time, then sit down and take the trouble to document all the times when you have been successful at this in the past. According to Leon Festinger, a psychologist who emphasised the role of tension in resolving conflicting thoughts, people tend to act in ways that are congruent with rather than contrary to their beliefs (study is cited in Hayes & Orrell, 1994). If you are persuaded that you can attain the standard you set for yourself, then you are more likely to invest the time and effort required to achieve your objective.

Checklist – Strategy for confidence-building on academic tasks

✓ Set a series of short-term goals that are achievable
✓ Write these down clearly
✓ Design a plan of work to complete each task within a given time
✓ Invest some daily effort to edge closer to your goal
✓ Tick off each task as you complete it
✓ Review your actions and process your successes
✓ Start the process with another task (you will now feel much more confident)

TIPS ON LEARNING FROM PAST EXPERIENCE

- **Take encouragement from previous improvement**

- **Ensure you can trace where the problems lie**

- **Set modest targets for improvement**

- **Allow time for positive changes to take effect**

- **Do not use improvements as a trade off for slumps in other academic goals**

Exercise – To summarise what you have learned in this chapter, write your own checklists on the following issues. These are designed to help you boost your exam confidence.

(a) Three things to work on that tend to drain your exam confidence:

✓ ....

✓ ....

✓ ....

(Continued)

(Continued)

(b) Three things that will feed your exam confidence:

   ✓ ....

   ✓ ....

   ✓ ....

SUMMARY

Chapter 4 summary points:

➤ Regular application to learning will develop your confidence

➤ Focusing on past achievements will feed your confidence

➤ Setting regular, reachable goals will increase your confidence

➤ Self-efficacy is belief in your ability to perform a set task successfully

➤ Confident belief in your own ability will lead you to action, effort and persistence

5 Turning Test Anxiety to Advantage

OBJECTIVES

What this chapter will give you:

➤ An introductory background to test anxiety research
➤ An ability to assess test anxiety symptoms
➤ Insight into how to benefit from anxiety
➤ Strategies to control the triggers of test anxiety

5.1 A well recognised and researched condition

There is no doubt that test anxiety is a very real phenomenon for many people. Large-scale studies have shown that students throughout the world have reported symptoms of test anxiety (Hembree, 1988; Seipp, 1991). According to these studies, high levels of anxiety are associated with, and are likely to have a negative impact on, test performance. The state of test anxiety cannot always be explained away by lack of work or exam preparation, for conscientious and highly motivated students also suffer from its debilitating impact (Zeidner, 1998).

Serious research on test anxiety has been going on since at least the middle of last century. Researchers such as Taylor (1953) attempted to measure test anxiety in students using self-report instruments. As the decades rolled on, measurement methods became more refined. First, Alpert and Haber (1960) showed that some of the elements of anxiety actually facilitated performance whereas other components debilitated it. Then Liebert and Morris (1967) highlighted the difference between cognitive and emotional components of anxiety, i.e. the difference between your thoughts during your test and the symptoms you experience such as trembling, perspiration, dry mouth, etc. The conclusion was that the thought factors were more likely to impair performance in an exam than the emotions (Deffenbacher, 1980). This was further refined into the untested assumption that negative thoughts about the exam were more detrimental to performance than distracting thoughts that were not related to the exam.

5.2 Check out test anxiety symptoms

In the diagnostic test below you are asked to estimate how strongly you would normally notice certain features in an academic test situation. You should do this retrospectively, based on your most recent experience of exams or tests.

Exercise – Diagnostic test of exam anxiety symptoms

These symptoms might be particularly applicable either before or during an exam, or in both. Circle the number that most appropriately describes you, according to the following code, and try to avoid the middle response (3) unless you are really unsure:

1 = Strongly disagree. 2 = Disagree. 3 = Neutral. 4 = Agree. 5 = Strongly agree.

1. During exam times I usually notice myself trembling   1   2   ③   4   5

2. At exam times I am prone to suffer bouts of nausea   1   ②   3   4   5

3. My regular sleep patterns are badly disrupted in the
    exam season   1   2   3   ④   5

4. During exams I sometimes feel somewhat breathless   1   2   3   ④   5

5. I notice an increase in perspiration (e.g. sweaty palms)   1   2   3   4   ⑤

6. My muscles are more tense than usual during exams   1   2   3   4   ⑤

7. I become aware that my mouth has dried up   1   2   ③   4   5

8. Exam periods are characterised by tension headaches
    for me   1   2   3   ④   5

(Continued)

(Continued)

9. I find it difficult to settle into reading the questions
   in an exam   1 2 3 ④ 5

10. Time in exams is lost for me because of panic attacks 1 2 ③ 4 5

Key to interpreting your score:

  Lowest possible score = 10

  Highest possible score = 50

  Scale midpoint = 30

A score above the midpoint represents an overall tendency towards anxious symptoms. A score below the midpoint represents an overall tendency away from anxious symptoms. You should also look at individual items (the midpoint score for each item is 3) as you may have a particular problem with several characteristics but these may not show up on your overall score.

One study tried to gauge anxious symptoms by attempting to take an actual physiological measure (see Sarason, 1984). The actual symptoms did not always correspond with students' own self-reported perceptions of their symptoms. This may not be such a big surprise because some students may give more attention to their symptoms and be more distracted by them than other students. Furthermore, other students may notice the symptoms less because they interpret them as positive cues for task-focused action. Therefore your own self-reported perceptions may provide you with more useful information than the 'scientific' approach.

5.3 Anxiety's disruptive function

Anxiety may have a disruptive function in a testing situation in that it is likely to interfere with your performance by distracting you from the task at hand and by blocking the clear recall of your learned material. However, it has been suggested that aspects of anxiety serve an adaptive function (i.e. they raise alertness and preparedness to challenges and dangers) in human survival (Spielberger et al., 1983). Animals can evade their predators when their nervous system is activated in time. If they fail to react in times of stress, then they become easy prey for the hunter. As humans we know when our autonomic nervous system has been activated. It happens when there is danger or a perception of danger and we need to take evasive action. The triggering of the autonomic nervous system is associated with symptoms such as trembling, sweating and a feeling of tension. It is the part of the nervous system that is activated temporarily to warn us of the need to prepare to meet a challenge or threat. The whole dynamic process is sometimes described as the 'flight or fight syndrome'. Another possible reaction to danger is to freeze on the spot like a helpless rabbit confronted with the headlights of an oncoming car. So although the autonomic nervous system is designed for survival, it can also be our undoing in stressful situations.

Illustration – An alarm that surpasses its usefulness

We can at times become excessively anxious when we do not need to be and a prolonged state of anxiety can take its toll on our health. Sometimes a car alarm is triggered by the wind or the smoke alarm in the house is activated when we are cooking. The continuous stimulus of loud and monotonous alarms can become an irritant – especially if the car alarm goes off in the middle of the night! Similarly, our autonomic nervous system, which was designed for a good, adaptive purpose, can go beyond its intended function to become an irritant at best and a block to progress at worst. There is a level of irritation that we can all accept as 'par for the course', but beyond that we look to redress the balance.

5.4   Tests: a regular aspect of human experience

It is impossible to go through life without some aspect of testing, whether this is a driving test, a job interview, a speech, a presentation, a media interview, a date or an academic exam. Three of the features that make tests distinctive are:

1. A component of evaluation

2. The importance attached to the consequences of performance

3. A time restriction with no opportunity to correct mistakes when the test is over.

The situation for the test anxious can be described using a flag analogy – a flag that goes up to signify that danger is present. There is the fear that you may not measure up to what is required, and with some students this interferes with their performance in an exam and can even block their ability to recall what they have learned (Covington & Omelich, 1987). Other people accept that testing is a necessary part of the human experience and take it all in their stride. Some can even interpret a few nerves as not a bad thing. Indeed, nerves may be perceived as a mechanism to preserve you from complacency and laziness.

There are some occupations where close public scrutiny is a constant and where individuals continually have to give an account of themselves. For example, politicians have to give regular press briefings and answer a bombardment of awkward questions, or the police have to give an account of crime control in a particular district. In many professions, such as health and education, there are regular audits in which practitioners must justify their regular work-related behaviours.

If nothing else, repeated testing at university may help you prepare for testing situations in your chosen career.

5.5 When the stakes are high

Illustration – A military exercise

In a simple military training exercise, recruits are required to walk across two parallel bars that have been elevated a few inches off the ground. They must walk across the full expanse of the bars without falling off. This is an

(Continued)

(Continued)

essential exercise in maintaining balance and there is no real danger associated with the task. A subsequent task is to walk across the same parallel bars over the same distance but this time the bars are raised to a higher level and thus there might be some danger in the exercise. You might imagine that there would be no difficulty with this, given that the recruits have already mastered the task. Surely the successful completion of the first task would give them the confidence needed to accomplish the same task again. It is evident, however, that the element of danger and risk that has been introduced may make all the difference to the recruits' confidence and ability to perform the exercise. For those who can focus on the task and keep a steady nerve, it may be just as simple as it was at the lower level (especially if it is indoors and wind is not a factor).

In the same way students with clear academic ability may falter when they are tested under strict time limits. The purpose of this chapter is not merely to help you identify the problem, but also to point you to the strategies that will allow you to give a good account of yourself and do justice to your exam preparation.

5.6 An enduring trait or a temporal state?

Exercise — What makes you anxious?

Tick any of the items below that are likely to make you feel anxious.

Visit to the dentist	......✓......	Doing a presentation	......✓......
Visit to the doctor	......✓......	Travelling by plane	....
A job interview	......✓......	A train journey	....
Meeting new people	......✓......	Going to new places	....
Doing a test or exam	......✓......	Wearing new clothes	....

(Continued)

(Continued)

Dancing before others	......✓......	Visiting a new place	....
Asking for a date	......✓......	Going on first date	....✓......
Checked by police	......✓......	Calling at a tutor's room	....

If you only ticked a few items, it is likely that this is 'state anxiety'. However, if you ticked a lot of items, then this is more likely to be 'trait anxiety'. State anxiety may happen in particular situations even if you don't normally feel anxious, whereas trait anxiety is the tendency to be anxious across a whole range of situations. Trait anxiety generalises over time and across situations, but state anxiety does not necessarily 'spill over' into other states. For some students, test anxiety is another manifestation of a more general problem, but for other students it is a problem that emerges in more limited situations (perhaps only in academic tests). Is test anxiety, then, a state or a trait, and does it matter? It could be argued that although test anxiety is a state, it becomes a trait for those students who experience it again and again. It may be that it is consistent for you across all testing situations and remains prevalent over time.

5.7 Symbolism in a flag

Army regiments used to carry their flag as they marched into battle and on it were the names of places where previous battles had been won. The flag was therefore a symbol of pride and encouragement so that the soldiers would not lose heart in the battle. However, they could be intimidated if they looked at the enemy's flag and found a similar list of success! For some students going into an exam, they may need to learn to redirect their attention to the 'right' flag.

As previously mentioned, the flag analogy can be used to describe test-anxious students. To them, an exam is like a dangerous event and to tackle it is a high-risk strategy. The thoughts that cause the 'wrong' flag to be observed are such things as:

- **The consequences of exam performance are serious**

- **The evaluation is crippling**

- **The blow to self-esteem through failure is intolerable to contemplate**

This may especially be the case for perfectionists, who are often in danger of setting standards so high for themselves that they impede their own progress.

> *It is still possible to do very well in an exam even if you get some things wrong – it need not be a disaster.*

5.8   Evidence to suggest a learning component

We have already seen that the symptoms of arousal can serve a purpose in our survival – they warn us of danger and call us to prepare for action. If we look at them from this perspective, we can interpret them positively, but if not, they can be a distraction from the task and a taxation on resources. Therefore what starts off as arousal (adaptive) can become anxiety (maladaptive). Maladaptive behaviours work to your disadvantage by turning you from the pathway that leads to your goal.

> *Stress is the body's call for action, but anxiety is a maladaptive response to that call (Covington and Omelich, 1987).*

Furthermore, it would appear that some aspects of the anxiety response have a strong learning component. Hembree (1988) reviewed 562 studies on test anxiety and concluded that the condition was not observed in first- and second-grade children, but began to emerge at grade three and was firmly in place by grade five. In other words, children start to become anxious as they begin to realise that they are being evaluated through tests.

A similar finding emerged in cross-cultural studies. In Arab nations such as Jordan, Syria and Egypt it was found that test anxiety scores were much higher than the world average, and test anxiety scores in Brazil were higher than those in the USA (El-Zahhar & Hocever, 1991). The researchers concluded that the different national scores reflected the fact that competition for university places in the Arab countries and Brazil (at that time) was strong and opportunities were limited. There is no case for concluding that the autonomic nervous system is more active in some nations than in others, but it does appear that test anxiety may have its roots in socially-constructed fears and competitive demands.

5.9   What's on your mind in a test?

Exercise — Worry about evaluation

All the items listed below relate to thoughts that might arise during a test. Circle the number that most accurately describes you, according to the following code:

1 = Strongly disagree. 2 = Disagree. 3 = Neutral. 4 = Agree. 5 = Strongly agree.

1.   I worry about what the marker will think of my efforts   1   2   3   (4)   5

2.   Memories of past poor performances enter my head   1   2   3   4   (5)

3.   I think that other students are doing better than me   1   2   3   4   (5)

4.   I wish that I had prepared better for the test   1   2   3   4   (5)

5.   I think that my exam strategy is very poor   1   2   3   (4)   5

23

Key to interpreting your score:

The middle score for the five items is 15.

Scores above this indicate a tendency to worry, and scores below this are indicative of a tendency to have overall worry under control.

Also look at your score on individual items – if above 3, this is indicative of worry.

As noted earlier, it has been found that thoughts during an exam do more damage to performance than physiological symptoms (the latter do not have to be interpreted negatively and therefore do not have to be a distraction). You will be able to control physiological symptoms in time; they cannot remain high forever. However, anxious thoughts (such as those suggested by the exercise above) distract attention from the task at hand and can divert attention into a self-defeating, negative, downward spiral. The way to deal with these thoughts may be simpler than you have imagined.

If you go into the test room armed with the realisation that distracting thoughts will impair your performance, you are already more than half equipped to counteract them.

You can, for instance, make a note that tells you to watch your thoughts and set it out in front of you. Or you can go back and read over the outlines you have completed in your rough work, or re-read the last paragraph you have written, to keep those self-defeating thoughts at bay.

5.10   What else is on your mind in a test?

Exercise — Irrelevant distracting thoughts

Circle the number on each item below that most appropriately describes your thoughts during a test, according to the following code:

1 = Strongly disagree. 2 = Disagree. 3 = Neutral. 4 = Agree. 5 = Strongly agree.

1.	I think about such things as TV, films and video	1	2	3	4	5
2.	My mind is occupied with worries not related to the test	1	2	3	4	5
3.	I find myself planning my activities (e.g. eating, dates, holidays)	1	2	3	4	5
4.	I relive conversations with others (pleasurable and/or annoying)	1	2	3	4	5
5.	My mind is occupied with recent news events	1	2	3	4	5

Key for interpreting your score:

The middle score for the five items is 15.

Scores above this indicate a tendency to be distracted, and scores below this are indicative of a tendency to have overall distraction under control.

Also look at your score on individual items – if above 3, this is indicative of distraction.

The items in the exercise above represent thoughts that are unrelated to the test. All distracting thoughts not related to the test can be classified as 'Test irrelevant thoughts', but the items above are non-evaluative whereas the previous cluster was evaluative in nature (i.e. directly related to the exam situation). One would expect that distracting thoughts which were related to the exam situation and were evaluative in nature would have a more detrimental impact on performance than distracting, non-evaluative thoughts (Deffenbacher, 1980; Sarason, 1984). However, this was an untested assumption. Our own research showed that both kinds of distraction were equally associated with poor performance in exams (McIlroy et al., 2000). This may simply be because both kinds of thoughts take up the time and energy that could be channelled into constructive answers.

Illustration – Don't get on the train

It may be helpful to think of distracting thoughts during an exam as being like a train that runs through your mind – a train of thought! If you decide to get on the train, your thoughts will run and run, and gather speed and momentum. When you see the train approaching, make the decision not to get on board, because the fare is too costly. If you have already boarded, then visualise the train slowing down, coming into the station and you getting off and leaving the station!

Ganzer (1968) found that those who lifted their head up and looked away frequently during an exam were more likely to perform more poorly than those who remained focused on the task. It is as if the students who look away have boarded the train and have decided to let the train run and run.

In one sense the process of being distracted during the exam is like physically leaving the test room – you might as well not be there at that time. If this happens to you, try to visualise yourself walking back into the room, sitting down at your desk and applying yourself to your task.

5.11   The power of illusions

A couple of Old Testament stories describe how two armies lost battles because of illusions. In the first story, the Moabites experienced a visual illusion. From a distance the reflection of the sun on the water looked like the blood of their enemies, who appeared to have been slain by others (2 Kings, chapter 3). This led to false security, complacency, drunkenness and, ultimately, defeat. The second is the story of how the Syrian army fled, leaving their tents, possessions and food behind, because its soldiers heard (an audible illusion) what sounded like a confederation of the Egyptian and Hittite armies coming out against them at night (2 Kings, chapter 6), and they fled. In both these stories the illusions worked against Syria and Moab, and in favour of Israel. If illusion can be strong enough, according to these old stories, to overthrow powerful armies, then their power should not be underestimated.

Although the beliefs some students hold about exams may be totally false, they still can have a powerful impact on behaviour because they are totally true in the minds of the students who hold them.

5.12   Bringing your thoughts under control in a test

The first illusion is that it is impossible for you to control your thoughts in a test. This is a myth and a lie that must be nailed.

You can refuse to get on the train even if you are already in the station and on the platform! Your mind is yours to control and can be tamed even if it appears to be like a wild horse that is determined to throw its rider!

Here is a checklist of the kinds of things you might want to do to keep your racing mind under control in a test.

Checklist – Factors to keep your mind under control in a test

✓   Write out the question you intend to address
✓   List the main points that you should be addressing
✓   Prepare a brief structure for your outline
✓   List names and dates that may be useful

✓ Work out and write down the time that should be spent on each point
✓ Write down any applied points that you could use
✓ If you have prepared any mnemonics, then write them down

If your mind is still distracted, then go through the same procedure for the next question. When you have completed your rough work, you can refer back to this every time you are tempted to drift.

Remember that simple mechanical actions such as eye focus and pen motion will assist in keeping you focused on the task in hand.

Once you start to write sentences, you will begin to feel more confidence and control. Whenever you do pause in your writing, watch that you are not tempted to look around you and then allow your mind to drift.

5.13 Bringing your emotions under control in a test

It is reported that an old Puritan made a covenant with his body in the following words: 'I will come with you three times a day to eat, if you will come with me three times a day to pray.' More recently, it has been claimed that it is not a bad strategy to sit down and write a letter to your own body (see Goud & Arkoff, 2003)! You can tell your body what you have done to look after it, apologise for the abuses, over-indulgences and neglect, and promise to try to correct these! The fact is that you are in control of your body and do not need to be entirely driven by it. The Puritan respected the needs of his body but was not prepared to let it take over his life and run the whole show! In the same vein, our emotions are very useful to us and their adaptive value is universally recognised, but like all bodily functions (or mind–body functions) they will dictate our every action if we let them.

Checklist — To keep your emotions under control in an exam

✓ Prepare yourself with a belief that you can control your emotions
✓ Do not feed them with uncontrolled, negative thoughts
✓ Try to interpret them positively as energy for performance
✓ Focus on the task before you rather than on distracting emotions

✓ Try some controlled breathing to slow down panic reactions
✓ Try out some muscle relaxation to reduce tension (e.g. gently roll your head five times to the right and five times to the left)

5.14 Prepare yourself as well as your material

In the next few chapters we will look at revision strategies and exam techniques, but at present the focus is on personal preparation in relation to thoughts and emotions in the exam. Of course the two can overlap in that if you are not adequately prepared for the exam, you are likely to leave a vacuum that anxiety may fill. That does not mean that all test-anxious students are malingerers – indeed, those that are very well prepared may be all the more anxious for fear that they will not do justice to their diligent efforts.

Those who are highly motivated to do well may fear that their drive levels will rise uncontrollably. Therefore part of your preparation is learning to keep your thoughts and emotions under control and channelling energy resources into producing good quality responses to questions.

Illustration – Plotting and tracking with focus on the ball

Athletes know that physical preparation is only half the battle and there is also a great necessity to focus the mind for the task. With wide television coverage of the last rugby world cup finals, more viewers became aware of how the players kicked a penalty or conversion from a 'dead ball'. The kicker would look up and down a number of times, focusing first on the ball and then on the spot between the two bars where he aimed to kick the ball. It is reported that one expert kicker aimed for a spot in the crowd behind the bars and kicked in that direction. The same focus and concentration can be seen in baseball where the thrower makes a few motions with the hand before the actual throw. He is finding his bodily stance and tracking the intended course for the ball. These sports competitors are highly professional and their movements are part of the psychological preparation that will enable them to be at their best and to capitalise fully on the talents they have.

5.15   A popular film with a useful moral

Illustration — Profiting from your Groundhog Day

In the film *Groundhog Day*, Bill Murray plays a character who re-lives the same day again and again, and has many negative experiences. However, he gradually learns to use these to his personal advantage and ultimately uses the events to win the love of his sweetheart.

At the beginning of your academic career, you may see your test and exams as a repetitive and dreaded 'Groundhog Day' that has too many negative associations. You may look back at much you have had to endure and forward to unpleasant experiences that you feel you will have to re-live. Like Bill Murray's character in the film, it is possible to change your perception and turn the repetitive situation to your personal advantage.

Look back over your past mistakes in tests and make sure you improve on them one by one and step by step. If you can improve on a few major factors within an exam each time, then you will doubtless improve your performance and achievement as you continue to develop.

Also, do not forget to focus on your strengths and encourage yourself with the skills and qualities you have acquired and developed. If you learn from your experience in increments, you will end up with the prize – not only an academic qualification, but also a range of skills that will make you a desirable employee.

Exercise — What to learn from your Groundhog Day (Exams)

Insert a number in each of the following items, according to the code provided below:

(Continued)

(Continued)

1 = Satisfied with my approach and efforts

2 = Room for a little improvement

3 = Need for substantial improvement

4 = Major surgery required

Being decisive	....	Engaging in effective revision	....
Reading the questions	....	Controlling wandering thoughts	....
Drafting the plans	....	Controlling my nerves	....
Planning my time	....	Omitting unnecessary 'padding'	....
Balancing my arguments	....	Problems with writing style	....

Unless you have scored all 1's, there is room for improvement. You should be able to identify the issues that need most attention.

SUMMARY

Chapter 5 summary points:

➢ Anxiety stems from a warning system that alerts us to danger

➢ Tests can prepare you to face future demanding roles

➢ Anxiety can interfere to block your best performance

➢ Symptoms of anxiety can be reinterpreted in a more positive light

➢ Awareness of intrusive exam thoughts is half the battle in beating them

6 Memory Techniques and Learning Principles

OBJECTIVES

What this chapter will give you:

➤ Exercises to highlight memory techniques
➤ Illustrations of memory skills
➤ Checklists that summarise learning methods
➤ Examples that bring learning to life

6.1   Basic building blocks

THE HARD FACTS

You cannot learn to read words until you learn the letters of the alphabet, and you cannot read or construct sentences in writing until you have learned the meaning of enough words to make overall sense of a statement, question or command.

> *Mere memory recall is not the ultimate form of learning but it is a necessary starting point that cannot be by-passed.*

If you do not possess some hard facts to start with, you do not have the building blocks to work with for more advanced learning and understanding. Of course you do not always need an in-depth knowledge of a given subject to understand basic written or spoken communication in that subject, but you do need to have retained enough facts in memory to have a 'working knowledge'.

For example, if you are learning another language you may be able to pick up the gist of a conversation between two speakers in spite of not being familiar with every word. Or if you are reading a very difficult chapter for the second time, your understanding will be greater than the first time for you will remember some of the difficult concepts from your first reading and this will facilitate greater fluency of thought. Each time you read over a chapter it should become a little easier and should take less time. What is happening is that you are making use of your memory to build your learning. If you understand this principle and practise it, your confidence in your ability to learn new material will increase and you will be less daunted by new challenges.

THE KEY TERMS

When hearing a lecture on a new subject for the first time you might be intimidated by the number of new terms that have to be used. For example, in your first lecture you might hear about 'empirical evidence', 'paradigm shift', 'prevailing zeitgeist' and 'anecdotal evidence'! It is an advantage if you have heard or read the terms before, and it will help if you write them down and at least try to pronounce them. Gradually, you can learn the meaning of each term and later you can learn about the connections between the ideas. Some of the new terms you learn may later become the key words that you may use as part of the outline for your exam revision.

Exercise — Take lecture notes or a book chapter or a journal article on a given subject and then follow the guidelines below.

- Make a list of all the major key terms
- Place a tick at those you have heard before
- Put two ticks if you can give a definition for the term
- Put three ticks if you can show the connection of the term with other concepts
- Insert an asterisk beside the words that are unfamiliar to you
- Devise a strategy for bringing all terms up to three-tick status (see the points below)

(Continued)

(Continued)

- Familiarise yourself with the sounds and pronunciation of the terms
- Gradually work on learning the meaning of each term
- Try to make a sentence that illustrates the meaning

6.2 Making the connections – the value of associations

Some memory researchers have concluded that memory trace (a deposit of information left in memory storage that can be detected and retrieved) is consolidated and the quality of learning is enhanced if you make connections between the various facts and if you can associate ideas within a network.

Illustration – A word game to play

In the game 'word associates', a group of people sit in a circle and one person will be nominated to start the game by verbalising their chosen word – e.g. 'trapeze'. They look at the person beside them as they speak the word, and that person must quickly and without hesitation find a word associated with the given word and then do the same with another person on the other side of them. The process goes on around the circle in a chain reaction until an individual is eliminated (because they delay too long or use an inappropriate word or repeat a word previously used). The game then resumes with the next person in line, and the exchanges continues round the circle in the same direction. As an example, from the word 'trapeze', the next word might be 'balance', followed by 'weigh' and then 'flour', 'bread', 'knife', 'surgeon', 'table', 'room', etc. After the game is over, prizes can be awarded to those who can recall and correctly trace all the words from given sequences. This last exercise is certainly a memory test, but it can also test one's ability to connect and make associations between words in a chain. In terms of preparing for an exam, this technique is invaluable. It is a useful practice to cultivate.

Exercise – Making efficient use of key terms from
a lecture or tutorial

- Identify a theme that may arise in your next exam
- Access the relevant material you have garnered from lecture notes, tutorials, seminars, textbooks, computer searches
- Identify a list of key words and familiarise yourself with them
- Learn the meaning of each key word
- Try to arrange them in a logical connection so that each will act as a trigger for the next
- When you learn new material see if your can 'hang it' on to the pegs provided by these terms
- Keep open to the need for adding new key words to your list

A worked example – Clusters of road and transport terms

Vehicles:	**Road rules (Drivers):**
Car	Insurance
Bus	Tax
Taxi	Safety (tyres, brakes, etc.)
Lorry	Alcohol & drugs
Motorcycle	Speed
Cycle	*Highway Code*

Traffic signs:	**Road rules (Pedestrians):**
Parking	Crossings (follow signs)
One Way	Pavement (walk on)
Speed	Codes (for crossing)
No Access	Risks (e.g. jay walking)
Dangerous Bend	Vision (check and take care)
Traffic Lights	Distractions (being careless)

6.3   Progress in memory work

Illustration – Shedding the skin

An old song described the metamorphosis of the caterpillar, shedding its skin (chrysalis) to 'find a butterfly within'. The butterfly is not destined to crawl along the ground, nor is it designed to remain as an unattractive creature (the caterpillar). Nevertheless, the 'ugly' period of time of hard work on the ground is the essential prelude to the time of beauty and freedom.

For the student, the early phase of learning provides the 'groundwork' for the more advanced and enjoyable phases. If you are persuaded that the information you are learning will become more enjoyable, useful and rewarding as you progress in your studies, you will be more motivated to continue. For example, if you are learning statistics, you may initially feel that the exercises are nothing more than meaningless number crunching. However, if you learn to apply statistics to real-life situations, there will be much more satisfaction in your endeavours because you will recognise the applied value of the exercise, as can be seen in the following example:

Example – Shock advertisements on the dangers of smoking: statistical strategy for testing their effects

Imagine that you decide to test the effects of shock advertisements on 50 smokers – what effect would the adverts have on the number of cigarettes smoked daily? You would note the average number of cigarettes smoked daily or weekly before and after the adverts. Just to be sure that any changes were not just by chance over time, you might also use a control group of 50 smokers who smoked the same average number of cigarettes but did not view the shock adverts. If you were really interested in the findings, the numbers would not be too difficult to remember because you are motivated to find out what exactly happened.

If there is a subject you really feel passionately about and would like to do a project on, you cannot just 'jump in at the deep end'. There is preliminary work that has to be done and basic facts that have to be mastered before you can do justice to your subject. On the other hand, you would not want to stay in kindergarten forever. Piaget observed that children's learning develops in phases (see chapter 2). If a quantity of liquid is poured from a long thin tube into a short broad jug, the quantity would remain exactly the same although it would not look as high. When children come to the stage of understanding this, they have acquired, according to Piaget, the ability to 'conserve'. In a similar way students can learn to widen their perspective by adding more facts to their repertoire of knowledge and adapt and apply their learning to diverse situations.

6.4   A context for learning – a shot in the light!

Educationalists have recognised that effective learning is more readily facilitated if a context for learning is provided (e.g. Ramsden, 1992). More often than not you will at least have some rudimentary knowledge that you do not, perhaps, give yourself credit for. If you make notes of what you already know (e.g. a list of summary words), you will have more confidence by seeing that you are not learning in a vacuum. In a worse-case scenario, you can at least bring with you the 'transferable' and 'generic' skills that you have previously developed. These might include such factors as computer and literature searches, the ability to take summary notes and to structure your learning material, and the ability to integrate and analyse the facts that you have obtained from your diverse sources.

6.5   Basic principles of memory – the four 'Rs'

It was at the end of the nineteenth century that Ebbinghaus (1885, cited in Hayes & Orrell, 1994) conducted his experiments on learning lists of nonsense syllables. On some occasions he and his assistant were able to recall the lists freely from memory. Later they found that even when they were unable to recall the lists perfectly, they did know if the words in the lists were not arranged in the original order and were able to reconstruct them into the correct order. In addition, they found that when they went to learn again the lists they had apparently forgotten, the learning was much easier the second time. To put this alliteratively, they used the four principles of:

- Recall

- Recognition

- Reconstruction

- Re-learning savings

Illustration – Giving directions to a driver

(This story will be used as a memory exercise later in this chapter — see 'Using hints to rebuild memories'.)

Imagine that as you walk to college or work, a car stops beside you and the driver asks you for directions. He has to move on quickly because he has stopped at a red traffic light in the rush hour and there is traffic behind him. He informs you that he has a job interview in 15 minutes and has already been round the one-way system twice. You know the place he needs to go to but, because of the one-way system, you do not want to send him off track. Perhaps feeling under a little pressure, you do not remember all the names of the roads the driver will have to take. But as you compose yourself you begin to think of the landmarks that will assist him to his destination. For example:

- He should pass a large Travel Lodge Motel in one road
- He should turn right into a road where the railway station is
- He can follow this road and take the second right after the hospital
- You then remember he will need to turn off to the left, after an electrical wholesale shop
- He then needs to turn left at the garage into the street that will bring him directly to his destination

You walk away feeling satisfied that you were able to give clear and accurate directions to an anxious driver who needed to get through an area that seemed like a maze. Then you begin to remember the names of the streets that you had temporarily forgotten under pressure. In effect, it did not matter that you had forgotten these, and might even have been an advantage, for the driver might have found it easier to identify the landmarks than the street names. What you did was quickly *recall* and *reconstruct* what you could. In the pressure of the situation you were able to fill in enough important details to give a successful description.

Compare this with a test situation where you are under pressure, and when you walk away from the test room you cannot change the 'direction' you have given. When in the test room remember that if you slow down and recall what you know, you will soon be able to fill in many of the details as the dynamics of associations in your memory are activated. Although some of the facts may initially come back to you in a somewhat dis-jointed fashion, you will eventually be able to reconstruct them in a coherent manner.

In a multiple-choice test or exam, you are tested on your ability to *recognise* the right answer and reject the wrong alternatives. Recognition refers to the process in which you recognise a statement or fact as familiar when you see it, but it does not come readily to mind through direct memory recall. Try the following examples (from information provided previously).

Exercise – Testing memory by multiple choice

Tick the correct answers in the following statements:

The researcher who conducted experiments on memory and nonsense syllables was

Ebbingclaus ...   Ebbinghaus ...   Ebbingberger ...   Ebbinghower ...

He undertook his research in

1884 ...   1984 ...   1885 ...   1985 ...

The correct answers to the tests are the second and third ones, respectively. If you could not identify the correct answers you will probably get them right if you try again in a few minutes! On some study programmes a multiple-choice exam may be aimed at testing your knowledge of a set textbook or just to test if you have familiarised yourself with a good range of basic facts across your topic. Although multiple-choice tests may not in themselves produce high-quality learning, some educators opt to use them alongside other assessment methods in order to ensure that students cover an adequate range of the course content.

Exercise – Using hints to rebuild memories

Try to recall the gist of the directions that were given to the driver going to the interview in the fictitious example provided earlier.

- Can you remember the landmarks that were used?
- Can you remember the order in which these were given?
- How many right and left turns were there?

Do not despair if you could not remember these. Few people will remember full details after one reading. But identification of certain facts (such as landmarks in the story) will help you build details and order around them.

In preparing for a multiple-choice exam, a good starting point is to read through all the set material just to get a good overall view. Each time you go back to read over the material again, you will have *re-learning savings* to work from and this will make your task less daunting. Of course questions can be set in a way that will test your understanding as well as your memory. It will be better for your learning if you try to work through problems rather than merely memorise the correct answers.

Illustration – TV Quiz shows and motivation to learn

Some contestants on television quiz shows acknowledge that they brush up on their general knowledge before they go on the show. They brush up on subjects

(Continued)

(Continued)

like geography, arts, music, films, cooking, spelling and any other theme they think might arise in the quiz. Their motivation for learning may be the large financial prizes that are available for winners. Another motive may just be the 'feel good factor' associated with doing well and the desire to avoid being humiliated under the gaze of millions of viewers.

If you are looking for motivation to prepare for a multiple-choice exam, then remember that this is a rare opportunity to pick up maximum or close to maximum marks. The multiple-choice test is the opportunity to boost your marks. Furthermore, it will provide you with a lot of the 'raw material' or 'building blocks' that you may be able to use in essay questions.

6.6   Variety of strategies – finding the optimal medium

Students can use a variety of strategies to aid their personal learning. However, if they are to get the most out of learning it is important for them to find the learning medium that suits them best. Some examples are:

• **Listening to suitable background music**

• **Working in quietness and seclusion**

• **Having a set time and place to work**

• **Varying both time and places of study**

• **Mixing any of the above**

• **Working in close proximity to others in the library**

• **Booking a library booth to avoid disturbance**

- Working in the open air (e.g. in a park or on a green)

- Working while using public transport

Eysenck (1995) found that students who are more extraverted prefer to study in the library near other students, and like to have their study punctuated with frequent breaks and opportunities to socialise. On the other hand, some individuals may prefer a set time and a set place (such as at a desk) where they can absorb themselves in study without distraction. A modicum of useful advice to each individual at this point is: 'Above all else, to your own self be true'.

One student explained that her optimal learning mode was to walk around her study while she verbally recited the information she had targeted for revision. Others might prefer to sit in a stationary position and, for them, making notes might trigger the recall of information in a chain reaction. Some have found that their concentration and focus are enhanced if they meet with a small group of fellow students and work through the material they are required to learn. Others like to learn at the lecture, tutorial or semi-nar through preparatory reading and strategic note-taking during the learning experi-ence. They then consolidate the material as soon as possible after the event.

Although students will have a preference for the strategy for structuring their own learning experience, there is no reason why a variety of methods cannot be integrated. These can be applied both to the initial learning and to the later recall and consolida-tion. It is also challenging and invigorating to try out new methods and approaches to learning as these can help to maintain freshness. Moreover, it is useful to process infor-mation in various modes, such as speaking, hearing, writing, discussion and drawing.

Exercise – Write out your own checklists of the following:

(a) The various methods that you can use in learning

    ✓ ....

    ✓ ....

(Continued)

(Continued)

✓ ....

✓ ....

✓ ....

(b) The advantages of using a varied approach to learning

✓ ....

✓ ....

✓ ....

✓ ....

✓ ....

6.7 Mind maps and motivation

Tolman (1932, cited in Hayes & Orrell, 1994) discovered that rats would learn to run a maze more quickly if there was a food reward at the end. Once their motivation was activated, the quality of their learning was increased. It is also a very good thing for humans to remind themselves of the value of learning. It may be helpful for you to document the reasons why you should learn. The Ulster Museum records a statement from the Irish writer, James Joyce, to the effect that the past existed for the present, and the present exists only for the future. These words have particular potency within the setting of a museum. They suggest that we have received a legacy from others and have a responsibility to pass this on. Such an understanding can provide motivation for learning. Here are some factors that you can use to motivate yourself:

- **Gaining respect from others because of your learning**

- **Passing on good influence to others (my children and future generations)**

- An appreciation of knowledge and understanding in their own right

- Returning something to my own parents

- Preparation for the professional career I anticipate

Illustration – A boys' game

As young boys a few of us became interested in cars and we all started to learn the makes and models until we could immediately identify each one on sight. It became a competitive game to see who was the first to identify a car type as it travelled toward us as we observed from the footpath. The first one to identify the car clearly would shout out, 'Vauxhall Viva', 'Ford Anglia', 'Morris Oxford', 'Austin Cambridge', 'Singer Gazelle', 'Mini Cooper', etc. (i.e. the cars that were common at that time). Sometimes we got it wrong because some of the models looked almost identical. We therefore, attempted to 'fine tune' our recognition abilities by studying shape, logo, etc. in more depth. Part of the motivation was the positive side of endeavouring to be the best in the group, and part was the negative side of ensuring that others did not leave us behind. There was also the longing for the future when we might be the owners of our own cars. Because we all aimed to possess a car one day, we already started to learn all we could about them.

What is most remarkable in retrospect is that all the boys in the little circle of friends got to know the names of all the cars and were able to identify them on sight. This illustrates the point that if you are sufficiently interested in what you are doing and sufficiently motivated, you are likely to do much better than you imagined. Often students are not highly interested in what they are required to learn and are not adequately motivated. Consequently, they do not learn and some conclude that they are not capable of learning. All the boys in our group learned the names, logos and features of the cars, although they probably all learned at their own pace. Many individuals show a great ability to learn things related to their own hobbies, interests and relationships.

Students often confuse their lack of motivation to learn academic work with lack of ability and thus do not invest the effort that would improve their performance.

6.8 Reproducing the material — organisation and integration

It is always difficult to try to learn a large range of individual items of information if these are unconnected. An example would be a range of random numbers such as 36, 75, 48, 23, 19, 53, 61, etc. One useful strategy is to use 'chunking', where the numbers are arranged into manageable clusters, like telephone numbers. According to G.A. Millar (1956), 7 is the magic number that most individuals can hold in working memory for a short time, that is 7 pieces of information or 7 digits. However, if a range of information is 'chunked' or compressed, then the potential for greater storage and capacity is increased. Furthermore, if the information is presented, say, as an interesting story, then the information will be more readily retained and recalled. Try out the following exercise to illustrate the point.

Exercise – Take two minutes to memorise the following list of words and take two further minutes to write down as many as you can remember.

Chimney	Number	Packet	Light
Cold	Stone	Biscuit	Violin
Table	Bracelet	Grass	Rain
Poster	Peanut	Horse	Phone
Metal	Skin	Donkey	Vehicle
Trinket	Monkey	Glasses	Bottle
Breath	Trolley	Waves	Jacket
Patio	Rust	Brolly	Window
Marker	Lace	Apple	Letter
Belt	Onion	Border	Cupboard

Take note of the number you have recalled and then try out the following exercise.

Exercise – Within the same time frames as the previous exercise, try to memorise the following list of words (it is not necessary to memorise the headings). Then take a sheet of paper and write down the four headings and see how many words you can recall under these headings.

Foods	Drinks	Vehicles	Cities
Bread	Wine	Car	London
Butter	Beer	Bus	Los Angeles
Pickle	Whiskey	Van	Glasgow
Cheese	Vodka	Bicycle	Belfast
Salt	Martini	Train	Dublin
Sauce	Sherry	Aeroplane	Cardiff
Peppers	Port	Motorbike	Paris
Mustard	Cider	Truck	Berlin
Beef	Lemonade	Tractor	Dubai
Onions	Cola	Crane	Tel Aviv

You should find that the second exercise was easier than the first, and this is because the information is organised under categories. If the material you are endeavouring to learn from a book or lecture has not been well organised, it will help the quality of your learning if you organise it into your own preferred format. In addition to clustering information into chunks, you can also employ other memory strategies, such as integrating information by visualising it. For example, in the food column in the exercise above, if you think of a sandwich (bread) that was buttered and contained beef, cheese and onions with peppers and pickles, then all you have to do was add salt, sauce and mustard and you have the perfect memory sandwich!

Another strategy is the method of loci. In this system you think of a journey that you regularly make and simply 'leave' the objects or ideas that you visualise at familiar locations on your journey. You can then mentally make the return journey and take note of the objects you have placed at familiar spots. In this way you will consolidate the memory trace by associating the new information with familiar information that is already systematically ordered in your mind. In the case of the list of cities in the exercise above, you can think of a round-the-world trip that covers the cities you have targeted to remember. You can also make the whole thing into a story where you travel from city to city by plane, eat several of those sandwiches on the journey and make a final journey between the last two cities by land using the various vehicles in the list (except perhaps the tractor and crane!). Furthermore, you may also think of sampling the various alcoholic beverages that are associated with the various cities, such as vodka in Moscow, wine in Paris, cider in London, whiskey in Dublin and beer in Berlin. In general, the more you can associate and integrate your strands of information, the better equipped you will be to learn effectively. For further memory techniques, see the complementary study guide, *Studying at University: How To Be a Successful Student* (McIlroy, 2003).

Exercise — Read over the following story once or twice.

Rachel, Fred, Sam and Sarah were so excited about their holiday in the Mediterranean the next day that they were afraid they might sleep in. Their worst fear happened when they slept through the loud clang of the alarm clock. However, there was still time to make it to the Airport five miles away for their scheduled 7 am flight. They decided not to shower or have breakfast and scrambled their four suitcases into the boot of the car and they were gone! It was 6.15 am on an early March morning and they hoped to avoid the heavy traffic. In the torrential rain, heavy lorries sprayed dirty surface water on to their windscreen. They resisted the temptation to overtake but it wasn't long until a clear, large, blue motorway sign guided them to the slip road for the airport. Worse frustration lay ahead! A farmer was moving his cattle across the road from one gate to another, and the cows were in no rush! A line of traffic quickly built up behind them in the narrow road and they realised that they were grid locked. They had no choice but to wait for 20 minutes until the cattle were all off the narrow road. When they arrived at the Airport they found a parking space near

(Continued)

(Continued)

the Terminal building but their flight was due to depart in five minutes and they still had to check in. Sarah and Rachel rushed on with the tickets and Fred and Sam quickly followed with the luggage. They discovered to their delight that the plane had been delayed for an hour and a half! Sarah remembered how angry she had been the last time her flight had been delayed. This time she was thanking her lucky stars. The four had time to relax and eat a postponed breakfast. When they boarded their flight they appeared to be the only passengers (from about 200 on the Boeing 737) who smiled at the airhostess through sheer delight at the delay! They looked forward with pleasure to their week in what they hoped would be warmer and less rainy weather in Spain.

Now try to recall as many words as you can within four minutes. (You have more time to remember on this occasion because there is much more information.)

The fact that the information is in story form may make easier to remember, although some students do better in the category task. Of course your memory of the story would be much better if you had designed the story yourself.

6.9   Six honest serving men

The six honest serving men refer to Rudyard Kipling's strategy for learning which comes in the form of simple rhyme:

I kept six honest serving men,
they taught me all I knew;
their names are what, and why and when
and how and where and who.

In other words, his secret of optimal learning was in the process of enquiry. Questions are the royal road to effective learning, especially if the questions are incisive. However, even questions that are initially misdirected may lead you back on to the right course. There is a growing emphasis in education on students developing the ability to learn independently. The unquestioned dissemination of knowledge in formal lectures is now regarded as inadequate in itself.

In a test or exam you are asked to answer the questions, but in the lead-up to the test the role is reversed – you have the time and freedom to pose the questions. Some text-books may have summary sections in which questions are set to guide your thinking either before or after you read. Sometimes lecturers will introduce their sessions with a series of questions that they intend to address in the course of the lecture. This is a very good way to help you to learn – it provokes you to think about various possibilities and to rule some of these out of the equation. Well-chosen and thought-provoking questions will help you to engage your mind by interacting with the topic. The following exercise on asking questions should not be attempted now – it is designed to get you into the habit of asking questions in your approach to lectures.

Exercise — Interactive learning in a lecture

Some lecturers may provide 'interactive handouts' that will already facilitate this process. If not, you may want to ask yourself the following questions:

- What are the learning outcomes of this session?
- What new material will I learn?
- What questions have not yet been answered?
- How is the theme of the lecture related to other themes?
- Is there a central, overall theme that can be summarised in a word or two?
- Are there several strands of thought around which I can group all the material?
- How might the material in this lecture be used in my assessments?
- Are there any interesting and memorable illustrations, applications or examples that will help make my learning more interesting and enjoyable?
- Can I restructure the content of this lecture into a skeleton outline that I can remember for revision?

Checklist – Learning strategy for approaching a book chapter

✓ Cut to the chase and pinpoint what I really need from this chapter
✓ Always read with pen and paper for brief notes
✓ Note the new words with which I need to become familiar

✓ Reproduce and (if necessary) restructure the major outline points into a format that best suits my learning goals

✓ Target the material I should highlight for use in my assessments

✓ Identify the content that dovetails with other aspects of my study programme

✓ Extract some short quotes that help to crystallise important points

✓ Note any new things learned and also what I have consolidated

✓ Identify points for further and fuller investigation

✓ Give a brief verbal summary of what I have read to a student friend

✓ Set aside time at the end of my reading session to consolidate the main points I have learned

✓ Make note of pages I might need to return to for revision

✓ Take note of the book's details (library reference) in case I need to return to it

6.10   Using clues to tease out latent memories

Illustration – Why crime scenes are reconstructed

The police frequently reconstruct crime scenes, including the events that led up to the crime, in the hope that the reconstruction will jog someone's memory, perhaps by the smallest of details. The police attempt to reconstruct the crime scene as closely as possible to the original (at the same time and on the same weekday as the crime itself). They often use an actor who looks like the victim of the crime and who dresses in the same kind of clothes as the victim was wearing at the time of the crime. If a car was used at the scene of the crime, then the police will use the same model and colour in the reconstruction. People who had been present in the vicinity at the time of the crime may suddenly be reminded of a small detail that could become vital evidence. Alternatively, the police may be able to piece together a series of small events to provide a much more accurate picture of what happened.

There are several similarities between academic work and forensic reconstruction:

- In reading over lectures notes, further details are recalled

- In complementing lecture notes with other reading, blanks will be filled in

- Through interactive engagement with learning material, dormant memories are activated and energised

- Through the ongoing process of learning and revision, a fuller and clearer mental picture emerges

- By nourishing initial learning, the overall mental picture becomes fresh and real

6.11   Learning to capitalise on context and association

If you watch a film for the second time, you will not ordinarily be able to recall the full details in sequence from start to finish. However, as you watch the movie, at various stages you will suddenly remember sequences of events that are about to happen. The more you have seen the film, the stronger the memory trace will be. The same principle can be applied to your favourite music albums. For example, you may have an album with 20 tracks. If asked, you may be able to remember 15 of the 20 tracks, but not necessarily in the correct order. However, if you play the album through, as you come to the end of each track it is likely that you will remember the track that comes next in the sequence. This is especially true if you enjoy the album and have listened to it a number of times. To use an analogy, you have set the train of memory in motion, and once you leave one station you will know what the next station is, if you are on your regular route. The encouraging factor from all this is that if you have the right context in which to learn and good associations with learning, when you come to do your exams, your memory dynamics will enable you to reproduce what you need to achieve your goals.

6.12   Keeping a toolkit of memory techniques

Very few individuals will have what is sometimes described as a 'photographic memory', but most people will be able to piece together enough of the picture to give a reliable impression of what an event is about. It should be remembered that strategies for memory must take two major factors into account – retention and retrieval. First, how can you input learning in an organised way? And second, what cues can you use to recall the material?

If a library is well organised under clustered themes, and with authors' names alphabetically arranged, then it will be easy to locate required books. Similarly, if you work your learning into clear content and link it together logically by association, your task of retrieval will be much simpler.

Exercise – Some of the tools that may help you in this process are listed below. See if you can briefly define each of them yourself but, if you need to, you can consult the definitions of these that are given at the end of the chapter.

Acronym ....

Alliteration ....

Association ....

Consolidation ....

Context ....

Levels of Processing ....

Method of Loci ....

Modes of Processing ....

Organisation ....

Reconstruction ....

Visualisation ....

6.13   Opening the secret chamber

In the British sitcom *Only Fools and Horses*, Uncle Albert loves to recall his war experiences, much to the annoyance of others! The impression is given that Uncle Albert has a rich repertoire of experiences to call on and that they are regularly activated by simple every day events. One is also left with the impression that these war stories are somewhat embellished for good effect! At university you will gradually accumulate a rich repertoire of knowledge and experience. When you walk into a test room you will bring with you, not only your knowledge of the subject, but also a wide variety of skills that will serve you well. In the current educational ethos there is strong emphasis on the importance of generic and key skills.

In your tests you will bring with you your ability to analyse, investigate and tease out conclusions with rigour. You will also bring personal qualities such as your confidence and motivation, and an ability to control your anxiety. Moreover, you will bring your cognitive skills, such as memory strategy, processing techniques and an ability to focus your attention.

By bringing all these qualities and attributes together in an exam, you will open up the secret chamber of knowledge that you have also brought with you into the test room.

Exercise – Write your own checklist of the range of skills and qualities you have already acquired or developed through exam experience (even if you feel you can still improve on these).

✓ ....

✓ ....

✓ ....

✓ ....

✓ ....

6.14   When memory goes wrong

Our sitcom character, Uncle Albert, may have embellished his war memories, but did he do this deliberately or had he come to believe his apparently exaggerated memories? The evidence would suggest that we sometimes add details to memories that are a figment of our imagination! In one study participants were requested to retell a story, 'The War of the Ghosts', but they tended to add details that they thought fitted the story. Therefore, we should be aware that memories can be faulty because we are selective in the material we attend to in learning, we may be prejudiced in what we choose to believe and we may suppress material with which we feel uncomfortable. However, apart from all this, we just sometimes get confused and merge ideas that appear to be similar but are really different.

Here are some simple steps that will help you to deal with memory interference:

- **Do not overestimate your memory and be aware that it can let you down**

- **Check out what you have learned by consulting several sources**

- **Attend small group sessions and discuss what you have learned with others**

- **Once you discover that you have had a wrong impression, make a note of this and focus on the correct alternative**

Checklist – Techniques you can employ to ensure that the quality of your learning extends beyond memory work to deeper learning

- ✓   Selective reading
- ✓   Focused note-taking
- ✓   Incisive questions (critique)
- ✓   Restructure the learning
- ✓   Make connections (integrate)
- ✓   Apply what you have learned
- ✓   Use problem-solving methods
- ✓   Make a story of the hard facts
- ✓   Use an adversarial approach – 'interrogate' the claims

Definition of terms (see exercise in section 6.12)

- Acronym — Using the first letter of a series of words to form one word such as: CAR (Competence, Autonomy and Relatedness).

- Alliteration — Using a series of words that begin with the same letter such as: 'Alliteration's Artful Aid'.

- Association — Associating one idea with another to process the original word at a deeper level.

- Consolidation — Going over your learning material again (as soon as possible after initial learning) in order to strengthen the memory trace.

- Context — Setting a topic into its order on your course or setting a particular point under its main heading in your topic. A second meaning of context is the environment in which you learn — it may activate your memory when you return to the place of original learning.

- Levels of processing — Moving memory work up into higher notches of learning, e.g. from memorising bare facts, to making connections between them and then to forming a story that includes all your basic facts.

- Method of loci — Visualising a journey you are familiar with, 'placing' your objects of learning at various familiar locations, and making the memory journey both ways so that you recall the targeted learning objects as you go.

- Modes of processing — Strengthening your learning through your senses, such as listening, speaking, seeing, reading and even feeling and smelling!

- Organisation — Organising the material you learn in a systematic way, e.g. through hierarchies, headings, subheadings, clusters, lists, etc.

- Reconstruction — Collapsing the structure of the material you have learned (e.g. lecture notes) and then reassembling it into your own preferred structure (e.g. composing an acronym or an alliterative phrase, or changing the order of the points so that you remember them more easily).

- Visualisation – Visualising a story or a drawing that will help you remember and connect your facts logically. The method of loci is one example. Some students use a colour code for running themes. For example, in an article or book chapter they may use green for one theme, yellow for another and blue for another. When they visualise the colour it helps them to remember the facts associated with a given theme.

SUMMARY

Chapter 6 summary points:

➤ Basic facts are needed as building blocks for learning

➤ Memory functions better when learning is structured

➤ Memory is improved when motivation and interest are present

➤ Memory efficiency entails using memory keys

➤ Memory work must lead on to deeper levels of learning

7 Revision

OBJECTIVES

This chapter will help you to:

➤ Prepare for revision from the beginning of the semester
➤ Structure material into extended and summary forms
➤ Organise material into forms that are easily retrieved
➤ Practise examples that will prepare you for revision
➤ Prepare yourself to enter revision mode

7.1   Buy a return ticket

A return ticket will often work out much cheaper than two singles, unless only a one-way journey is planned! In your academic work you will definitely need a 'return journey' to pass again through the material you have previously encountered. Without a 'return ticket' for your university work, you will find that the return ride is much more expensive than you had envisaged. In the last chapter, it was emphasised that you should not underestimate your memory. However, it is also important not to over-estimate your memory – give it a chance to function at its best by your good planning and organisation. If you make no plans to revisit your course material until your exams are imminent, you may be appalled at how vague your recollection appears to be.

7.2   Plan for each learning activity

It should be your aim to spend a moment or two at the end of each learning activity to make a few points that you can take away with you and use. The more succinct the points, the more likely you are to glance at them periodically. It may help to frame a few questions that you can use in relation to:

- A lecture

- A seminar

- A discussion

- A tutorial

- An experiment

- A journal article

- A book chapter

- A computer search

You may, for example, ask:

- What are the main points? (A word or two for each)

- What are the important names of researchers, scholars, theorists?

- What aspects of this are new to me?

- What do I need to follow up on and develop further?

- How can I relate this to other aspects of the module?

- How can I relate this to the study programme more broadly?

- Does this have any direct or indirect bearing on my exams or course work?

It is better if you can design your own questions, but these might act as a catalyst to get you started. Moreover, it is wise to transfer some summary notes into a notebook or on to revision cards. This practice will help you to strengthen the memory trace and to process the information more thoroughly, and will provoke you into thinking in more depth on the subject.

If you do not make the task of taking brief summary notes too laborious, you are more likely to make a regular commitment to this good practice.

Remember that you should aim to be an active participant rather than a passive recipient in your education.

7.3 Highlight the landmarks

Revision should, in effect, begin as soon as your course commences, or you should at least begin to prepare for the later time when you will devote yourself to revision.

There is much to learn from the squirrel that stores up nuts for the winter. It is not only essential to revise for your exams, it is also vital that you prepare adequately for the season of revision.

Illustration – The analogy of a journey

If you take note of the landmarks on an outward journey, you will be able to navigate your way back with greater ease. For example, if you are driving a car, you will want to be familiar with the names of the towns and villages that you have to pass through to reach your destination. You will also aim to prepare in advance for meeting motorway signs, slip roads, lanes, etc.

By the time you come to do your revision, the subject matter should bring you more than a vague feeling of *déjà vu* – you should be clearly and consciously aware of your study territory. Although there will inevitably be some fresh material to absorb during the revision process, it is not a good time to commence climbing the mountain of learning.

Total unfamiliarity with the subject at such a late stage might be the trigger for panic and anxiety, especially if you only begin to address your task very close to the exams.

It is said that procrastination is the thief of time, and it will certainly rob you of the opportunity to prepare the quality responses to questions that you will need. It need not be a daunting task to prepare some 'landmarks for revision' as you journey through your study programme. This chapter gives you guidance on features such as bullet points, headings, major and minor themes, etc. These are the elements that will give structure and content to your revision, and will also provide you with a feeling of mastery and direction. You will, if you follow this guidance, feel a sense of control over your own academic destiny, and you will have equipped yourself with some of the tools that will help counteract anxiety and tension. Just a small amount of motivation on your journey will give you a sense of empowerment to accomplish your goals.

To prepare some revision landmarks you could:

- **Note and learn a list of key words**

- **Read over material as soon as possible after initial learning (consolidation)**

- **Develop a system of mnemonics (see Chapter 6 on memory)**

- **Work out linkages between your points**

- **Design major headings and subheadings (see example below)**

- **Examine how the learning material can be applied**

Below is a worked example to illustrate the use of headings and subheadings.

A worked example — Political battle for the hearts and minds of the electorate

1. **Tactics for the government**

a. Set election at a time when the economy is healthy
b. Time election for when opinion polls favour the government
c. Ensure pre-election budget is sound, balanced and gives feel-good effect
d. Publish a manifesto with sound policies on major issues with effective sound bites

(Continued)

(Continued)

2. **Strategies for the opposition**

a. Target all marginal constituencies for concerted campaign
b. Highlight government shortfalls on previous electoral pledges
c. Produce realistic spending targets that improve public services and individual wealth
d. Articulate realistic alternative policies across major issues

3. **Decision for the electorate**

a. Which party has most earned the right to be trusted?
b. Which party has presented the most realistic agenda?
c. What are the major policies on health, education, economy, crime, defence, home and foreign affairs?
d. Is there a dilemma in choosing between the preferred party and the quality of the local candidate?

7.4   Full notes and summaries

If you are required to write lab or scientific reports, you will be aware of what an Abstract or Summary is. In an Abstract you are required to write a limited number of words (e.g. 100–150), and you are expected to summarise in a sentence or two the major conclusions from all the sections. The goal is to remove all the details, include only what is essential and crystallise your material into the bare, central findings or conclusions. From this you can then convert your Summary into bullet points that will serve as a skeleton for your revision. That does not, of course, mean that you should discard your full notes. You can read over your headings and subheadings before and after you read over your full notes. On other occasions, such as travelling on the bus or train, or during a boring wait in a queue, you might choose to browse through your summary notes and headings over all your targeted topics.

Here is a worked example.

A worked example – The MMR jab

Read over the following summary of a debate on the MMR jab and
then note down the bullet points that might act as pegs for remembering
the content of the discussion.

Over recent years there has been a big scare with the MMR (Mumps, Measles,
Rubella) jab for children, and this has been related to the onset of autism. A tiny
minority of children develop autism after receiving the MMR jab. Several problems
have aggravated the issue, and these have included scares about other diseases
(e.g. CJD), questionable government statements on other health issues (were the
government motivated by an economic agenda?) and the role of powerful drug
companies with a vested interest.

A compounding problem is that autism may emerge at an age that just follows the
prescribed time for the MMR vaccination (i.e. even in children who have not had
the jab). Most children who have the jab do not develop autism, but scientists will
not normally say that any drug is 100 per cent safe. The absence of this language
should not necessarily lead to panic or suspicion. In conclusion, the reality is that
we always take calculated risks (e.g. with food), but in the present example
parents must weigh the issues and take the decision on behalf of vulnerable
children. The alternative, however, might lead to epidemics in the diseases that
the MMR jab was designed to counteract.

You could use the topics below to arrange your revision notes:

- Statement of the problem
- Political aspects
- Scientific arguments
- Moral issues and responsibilities
- Emotional facets
- Complications and dilemmas
- Risk balance probabilities

*The secret of good revision is to alternate between the fuller version of the story and the sum-
mary points. After practice, you will be able to make stronger links between the two methods.*

7.5 Processing and problem-solving

Processing refers to engaging your mind with the material you are learning at a level that is higher than memory work. Processing requires you to think, question and analyse the claims that are made. One way to do this is through problem-solving, or problem-based learning, which includes both asking and answering questions. For example, does what you are learning provide a good explanation to the questions and problems you raise? Learning to question and analyse the issues you are studying takes time and practice. So be patient with yourself and set some modest targets initially if you are not used to this approach. Always be on the look out for a problem-based approach in your lectures and textbooks, and make a note of these so that you can later use them in your revision.

Illustration – Advice from a piano tutor

A piano tutor gave some sound advice to her pupil as he was preparing for his music exam, specifically with reference to playing scales. She suggested that if he practised too much, he would learn the scales so well that he would merely play them from memory rather than read them directly from the music sheets. This would inevitably lead to lapses in memory and therefore errors in practice. Although memory is an essential part of learning, it is not the only tool to be used, and over-reliance on it can impair the quality of learning.

The moral of the story is that revision should be more than a memory exercise. Errors will creep in if revision becomes monotonous through humdrum repetition. Leave yourself some work to do at the revision stage and this will keep the activity fresh and interesting.

An example may be a problem-solving activity in which you have to work through logical steps to arrive at a solution. Or you may try to add a new aspect to your revision work, such as processing information in a different mode. For example, you could draw out your points in the form of a flow chart or path diagram rather than as a bulleted list (see Chapter 9, section 9.6). Educationalists claim that quality learning is not achieved by memory work alone. They argue that higher intellectual activities, such as understanding, analysing and establishing connections between points, are also required. Developing these skills will keep your revision fresh, especially if you try to approach the problems from a variety of angles. For instance, the example of the MMR jab above requires thinking and understanding as well as remembering the facts.

7.6   Capitalising on re-learning savings

Illustration – The third most recognisable man in the USA

In a television documentary that was a tribute to the late country singer, Johnny Cash, it was stated that he was once the third most recognisable man in the USA after former President Nixon and John Wayne. This suggests that his face was so often seen in the media that people could quickly identify him, even at a glance. A famous UK celebrity, David Beckham, was so often in the media that he was instantly recognisable from various angles. On one occasion advertisers used the silhouetted profile of his face and distinctive hairstyle and the whole nation knew who the advertisement referred to!

It is clear from these illustrations that the human mind has the capacity to recognise instantly familiar subject matter, but this remarkable ability is not confined to visual images. When you have learned your academic material sufficiently well, it will be encouraging for you to look at your textbooks and journals and instantly recognise the 'familiar territory' of that material. It will help you to build up your confidence and enhance your knowledge base. Furthermore, when you enter the test room and see the exam questions you will feel confident because you will know that you have the deposits of knowledge to address the questions in front of you. The process of revision will help you consolidate what you have learned. Motorbike racers find it easier to navigate the race track once they become familiar with the bends, bumps, humps, hills and hazards. The more familiar you are with the study material before revision commences, the easier you will find it to work your way around 'the track'.

7.7   Organisation and planning

Organisation and planning are all about getting into the regular habit of compiling and storing information in places where you will be able to retrieve them easily at the time when you really need them. The consequences of not doing this are:

- **Time is wasted in trying to locate the material**

- **Sources of important information are misplaced**

- **Sources of important information are forgotten**

- **The same quest to acquire information is repeated two or even three times**

- **Panic, frustration, guilt and anxiety**

Checklist — Practical steps to compile information

✓   Keep a folder for each module
✓   Use colour codes for each subject and topic
✓   Label each folder clearly
✓   Use subject dividers for each theme or topic (colour code and label)
✓   Have a table of contents page at the beginning
✓   Add material from various sources to the appropriate sections
✓   Earmark your acquired material for its 'destination'
✓   Avoid treating notes on scrap paper with contempt and transfer them to permanent storage
✓   Use a   pocket notebook for revision that corresponds with each folder for your revision notes
✓   Keep folders together in a place where you will find them, and always return them there
✓   Check each night which folders you will need to carry to university on the next day and pack these into your bag

7.8   Marking the revision zone

Some people regularly put off dealing with problems, using the old adage that 'we will cross that bridge when we come to it'. As we have clearly seen, this is not a good principle to apply to revision.

The quality of revision will be diminished if the revision period is not planned for. Therefore, it is sensible to have a set date that marks the official beginning of revision.

Illustration – Changing thinking mode at the border

Consider the analogy of crossing over a border into another country. The driving laws may be different from those you are accustomed to, for example the speed limits may differ and you may have to drive on the other side of the road. Drink/drive laws, laws for braking distances, tyre-depth requirements might all be totally different. Once you enter the new country you may have to go into a different mode of thinking in many respects. Sometimes entering another country means changing time zones. When a ship crosses the International Date Line, for example, the crew and passengers must add or subtract a day according to the direction in which they are travelling. If it happens to be your birthday, you could find yourself celebrating twice or missing it entirely!

If your mind does not go into 'revision mode' when you enter the 'revision zone', you will fail to capitalise on the benefits that can be extracted from this time.

7.9   Conditioned for revision

Another analogy that can be used is related to the problem of insomnia (and this example may also have practical benefits for those who develop the problem!). Under normal circumstances you are conditioned to sleep at given times and in a particular place, but what do you do if you cannot sleep when you go to bed at night? One answer may be to compile a list of problems in order to find the culprit(s).

- **Drinking too much caffeine at night**

- **Your mind is over-worked and saturated in the late evening**

- **Eating large meals late at night**

- **Sleeping at other times and throwing the body rhythm out of synchrony**

- **Associating bed with other activities, such as reading, chatting and watching television**

- **Insufficient exercise and fresh air**

In this searching process you want to examine all the possibilities to ascertain how to restore normality and balance to your daily life. Some students may feel that revision is almost as 'unnatural' as insomnia. Revision involves a suspension of many of your usual activities and an intense degree of focus on study. However, your aim should be to approach revision with a view to adapting it into your programme in as normal a manner as possible. For example, think of the frame of mind you go into for work, leisure, holidays, exercise, Christmas, socialising, etc. Accept that revision is just another time like these when you adapt the mode and maintain the momentum.

Revision is only for a very short period of time and you can treat yourself with some well-earned rewards when you 'emerge from hibernation'! When you get used to this way of thinking, an instinct will kick in when you begin the revision process. For example, when a person experienced at word processing is typing at the computer, he or she does not consciously think of where to locate each character. The positions of the keys have been so well learned through practice that the typist can concentrate fully on the content of the material with which he or she is engaged.

7.10   Pacing and timing

The best way to examine this aspect of revision is to take a worked hypothetical example for summer exams.

Worked example

Final teaching week ends on Friday, 30 April
First exam (2 hours) – Monday morning, 17 May
Second exam (2 hours) – Wednesday morning, 19 May
Third exam (2 hours) – Friday afternoon, 21 May

Revision Phase A – Preliminary check out

- Step 1 – First weekend: Check out that all revision materials are intact and ready
- Step 2 – Work out revision timetable for the next two weeks
- Step 3 – Engage in some relaxing and enjoyable activities over the weekend with the promise to self that revision mode begins in earnest on Monday morning. Do some 'work outs' on preparing your motivation (e.g. lay out the materials you will need and begin to mention to friends that you are scheduling revision)

Revision Phase B – First full week

- Step 1 – Have a set time to rise, have breakfast and commence work for each day from Monday to Friday (include places to study; travel time may also need to be factored in)
- Step 2 – Each night (or at the end of the study day) set aside all the materials to be used on the next day
- Step 3 – Decide if you need to be in one location or to vary these (e.g. at home in the morning, the library in the afternoon and some recap at a café in the early evening)
- Step 4 – Plan breaks for coffee, lunch and evening meals. Find some room for relaxing activities later in the evening, especially in the first week
- Step 5 – In the first full day of revision it may be useful to peruse all your materials in order to get a feel for where you have to go over the next few weeks
- Step 6 – Be aware that you have three exams and must have a systematic plan to do justice to preparing for each one. Also it may be sensible to revise in the same order as the sequence for the exams
- Step 7 – Avoid alcohol (or restrict your intake) and avoid caffeine late at night

Get your body into a good steady rhythm of rest and work.

Revision phase C - Second weekend

- Step 1 — Plan your revision activities for the next week (over the weekend) — it may consolidate these plans if you write down times, places, breaks, etc.
- Step 2 — Briefly revisit outlines from the last week
- Step 3 — Take some time out at the weekend so that you can feel really fresh on Monday morning. Do some 'work outs' on preparing your motivation
- Step 4 — Remember that excessive alcohol consumption at the weekend can upset your rhythm and momentum for the beginning of the next week

Revision phase D - The second week

- Step 1 — Follow the same routine as the previous week and build up momentum
- Step 2 — You may now feel better equipped for your study and revision sessions
- Step 3 — Allow some time to be with your fellow students for the exchange of ideas and identification of problems (you may prefer to start this in week 1)

Adopting similar routines is the best way to plan and time your revision schedule.

7.11   Carry your cards

In recent years the use of small cards, which can be conveniently carried in a wallet or purse, has become a widespread practice. People commonly carry debit and credit cards, donor cards, business cards, customer loyalty cards, etc. These serve the practical purposes of simplicity and convenience. Long before the current popularity of cards, students have been using them as revision aids. Revision cards can be numbered, given a title, and can list the central points of a particular topic. They can also be carried conveniently in your pocket or bag, and used when you travel on a bus or train, or while you are in a queue or waiting around for a friend.

> *Think of the time that you waste waiting around and how this could be usefully employed in scanning summary notes.*

Notice how people become impatient and frustrated with long queues, for example at the check-out in the local supermarket. Think of how you can save yourself from these negative, counterproductive reactions and think of how many revision cards you can work through in this time!

The use of cards may be appealing to some students while others may prefer a small pocket notebook. Whatever your preference may be, the important issue is to document your main outlines in summary form so that you can scan these at a convenient moment and in a short period of time. Look back at the worked example on government elections near the beginning of this chapter to see how revision headings and subheading can be used in your revision cards. If you have your own 'portable revision system' to carry around with you, you will be able to keep in touch with your subject matter at regular intervals. This is a good habit to cultivate, not just during the revision period but also in your academic programme more generally.

Illustration – Driving on the wrong side of the road!

In the UK and Australia, traffic travels on the left side of the road in contrast to Europe and the USA where vehicles must travel on the right side. If you are driving in a country where the traffic travels on the opposite side from what you are used to, it would be better to comply than defy, even if you think that it is really everyone else who is on the wrong side of the road! Most individuals would not deliberately flout the law in this manner but it is conceivable that some might forget and lapse into the routine they are used to. Some advice given in a motoring book to prevent this happening is simply to tie a little cloth around the steering wheel. This would be a constant reminder that you are in another country and must comply with different rules.

Think of the revision time as the period when you must keep your reminders before you by carrying them around so that they are always within easy reach. Furthermore, your revision cards (or your revision outline notebook) must incorporate both an outline structure for your topic, as previously suggested, and a list of the points that you have 'tweaked' in various forms to allow some flexibility in how you might approach various exam questions. This will be developed further in the next chapter.

7.12   Use of past papers

There is a real advantage in looking over exam papers from previous years, especially from recent years, as part of your revision programme, but ensure that you look at a variety of these and not merely one. Looking at previous exam papers will help you to think critically about your subject matter and will sharpen your awareness of what is required of you in an exam. Moreover, it will enable you to envisage a range of draft outlines in your revision so that you can process and 'spin' your material in a number of different directions. Tutors will usually put a particular angle on a question and this may be a variation on a previous angle or even on a combination of previous angles. It is therefore a very good exercise to peruse past test papers and to try to imagine new angles that might emerge. The latter strategy can be adapted with reference to your course content and outline. This issue will be addressed again in Chapter 8 with reference to the exam itself but at present the emphasis is on revision. The important point here is to make sure that you can learn your outline points in a manner that will allow you to modify their order, emphasis and orientation.

Example – A theme on nutrition

- Various diets go in and out of fashion (e.g. Atkins)
- Food consumption is complicated by food scares (e.g. CJD)
- There is also a debate about genetically modified (GM) foods
- In previous decades the debate about additives, preservatives, colours and flavourings was prominent
- Another health-related issue has been sodium levels in food
- A further aspect has been methods of cooking and cooking utensils
- Surrounding issues include junk food and the promotion of junk food by celebrities
- There is the issue of school meals and convenience foods for children
- Other related issues include anorexia nervosa and bulimia
- Nutritionists emphasise food combining and balance
- In western societies gender pressures have been for the slender woman and the muscular man

The exercise below will require a little time and effort to complete, so feel free to jump over it or to read quickly through it so that you can benefit from the point it is making. You may consider doing this exercise in groups as a course exercise.

Exercise – Suppose that nutrition has been part of your course and that the themes listed above were covered in your lectures. Now complete the following tasks:

- Pick out or think of a word or two that would summarise and remind you of each of the points above (e.g. 'Atkins' for the first point)
- Can you arrange these words in a form that would be easily remembered (e.g. a mnemonic)?
- If you start to write the summary words down, you may find that the inspiration will begin to flow
- Look at the following questions and see what material you can arrange around it (watch that you do not strain and force material that is irrelevant)

1 Critically assess fashions and fads in food.

2 What impact do food scares have on eating patterns?

3 Suggest how the battle against poor diet can be won.

4 Evaluate whether any campaign to improve the eating habits of the nation should give attention to gender.

5 Discuss whether children should be targeted directly in the battle to reduce junk food consumption.

6 Critically assess the role of media and celebrities in setting trends in the nation's dietary habits.

It is not difficult to see how the above questions will help you to think about the previous 'course outline'. They will help you to look at your material from various angles and with different emphases.

It is important to use thinking strategy as well as memorisation in your revision strategy.

7.13   Revising with others

It makes a lot of sense to set aside a few periods of revision time with your friends as your exams are approaching. Of course, this has to be by mutual agreement and everyone should be prepared to make a contribution. If done wisely, it can be a stimulating experience that brings benefits to all those involved. It should not, however, be an opportunity for lazy students to 'cash in' on the hard work of their friends, and for conscientious students to end up feeling that they have been used and abused. Therefore, choose friends who are prepared to 'put their shoulder to the wheel'. Engagement in revision with others must never be seen as an alternative to personal revision, but when the two methods are employed in parallel, the benefits can be enormous. These are outlined below. These benefits will be maximised if everyone is given a task beforehand to bring to the collective effort.

ADVANTAGES OF REVISING WITH OTHERS

1. A variety of emphases and angles are brought to the discussion.

2. A wider range of materials can be accessed and mutually exchanged.

3. Grid-locked problems can be resolved.

4. You can gain a greater awareness of where you have fallen behind or have misunderstood material.

5. You can receive reassurance when you are on the right lines.

6. You can gain a feeling of solidarity with others.

7. Cultivation of working in a team is deemed to be an employability quality.

8. You can process your material at a deeper level and in a variety of modes.

9. You can be challenged to defend your position.

10. You are motivated to learn before and after each session (setting goals and targets).

11. There is a division of workload with others.

12. New vistas of thought are opened to you.

SUMMARY

Chapter 7 summary points:

➤ Learning material should be earmarked for the later 'return' journey

➤ Headings and subheadings will provide templates for revision

➤ Balance revision between outline overviews and extended reading

➤ Set yourself some problems to work through during revision time

➤ Use past papers to complement your other resources

➤ Set a date that marks the beginning of going into revision mode

➤ Working with others can help motivate you in revision

➤ Work out a revision timetable that will make revision effective

8 The Exam

OBJECTIVES

This chapter will help you to:

➢ Attend to the practicalities that help keep panic under control
➢ Use your exam skills and resources to maximum advantage
➢ Practise task and time management activities
➢ Target exam questions quickly and efficiently
➢ Adapt your memorised outlines to your exam needs
➢ Identify exam distractions that weaken your performance
➢ Learn to keep your mind 'on task' in an exam
➢ Practise examples for addressing exam questions

8.1 The big day

A wedding is often described as 'the big day'. The expression can also be used to describe a cup final or graduation, etc. The term is reserved for important or momentous occasions and your test or exam is important because it represents the climax of your efforts in relation to the subjects being tested. Another feature about a big day is that you mark it out well in advance – it stands out in the calendar and you know when it is approaching.

Unfortunately some students look towards their exams with fear, dread and anxiety. This can lead to repression of exam thoughts and therefore suspension of revision. In order to change such a negative mindset it is important to face the problem head on.

Once you start to engage in revision and use the strategies outlined in the previous chapter, you will feel a sense of control over your study material. As your confidence grows it will be possible to begin to look forward to the exam day with more confidence and positive beliefs about yourself. A 'big day' can be viewed as one that will have a celebration at its climax, and you can be assured that your efforts and preparations will give you some control over how you will feel at the end of your test day. A well-planned wedding is more likely to be much smoother than one that is not adequately planned.

8.2 Preparing the practicalities

One of the things that can trigger or aggravate exam nerves, tension and obsessive thinking is the failure to give due attention to the simple practicalities associated with the exam. This can be counteracted by making an advance checklist of all the things that you should have in place on the day of the exam. The following list is typical of the things you should endeavour to remember. You could pin up such a list at your place of residence and begin to glance at it as the exam season approaches.

In the points that follow throughout this chapter you will notice that there is a mixture of academic and simple, practical issues – both are needed if you are to be at your best on the day.

Checklist – Exam practicalities

✓ Check and double-check the time and place of the exam
✓ Leave plenty of time for your journey
✓ Make sure you have all the relevant stationery that you will need
✓ Bring some water if you are likely to need this
✓ Take your revision notes on the journey
✓ Ensure you have sufficient money or a ticket for travel if relevant
✓ Take watch to plan your division of labour by time

It is not uncommon for people who are anxious to forget basic things.

8.3   Arriving with the right mindset

Illustration — The 'wow!' factor in the Olympic ceremony

In the run-up to your exams there are a number of things that you can do that will help you prepare for your test. When the Olympic Games open, the atmosphere has got to be right on the day. The organisers can put all the mechanics of the operation in place for the opening ceremony with efficient organisation and planning, but they also need the dynamics of atmosphere, and only the crowd, in response to the ceremony, can provide that. Atmosphere can also be transmitted to a worldwide audience through television and radio broadcasting. In spite of all the preparation and planning, the inspiration of the occasion has to be there at that very moment, and of course the two things will invariably go hand in hand.

But the inspiration does not come without the perspiration!

At the opening ceremony there is the colourful display of the flags of the participating nations. Along with this there are fireworks, music, singing etc., but also the spontaneous reaction of the crowd with cheers and applause. It is often the case that actors are inspired by the reaction of the audience and are spurred on to give the performance of their life. They feed off the atmosphere and the flow of adrenalin. In order to ensure that you are at your best, and can capitalise on the flow of inspiration on the day of the test, check that the following ingredients are in place.

Checklist — Ingredients for optimal test performance

- ✓ Good revision strategy planned over the whole semester
- ✓ Sound mnemonics that include outline plans
- ✓ Awareness of exam structure — e.g. the number of questions presented and number to be answered
- ✓ Plans for time allocation for each question and each section of a question
- ✓ Ensure that all practical necessities are planned for

✓ Aim for a good night's sleep on the eve of the exam
✓ Avoid alcohol around exam time
✓ Talk to yourself on the morning of the test (it is better than listening to yourself)!
✓ Interpret arousal as positive energy for your test
✓ Focus on the task and get your mind into gear!

8.4 Controlling the ANS symptoms

It is important to know that the symptoms that arise after the autonomic nervous system (ANS) has been activated can be controlled to some extent. These symptoms can be interpreted as cues for action. If you interpret them negatively or 'freeze' in response to them, you will impair your performance through distracting thoughts. ANS symptoms include such things as trembling, breathlessness, panic, tension and palpitations. These cannot stay too high for too long and must eventually come down. As you focus on your task and are preoccupied with your goals, you will not notice ANS activity to the same extent as before. You will feel a greater sense of control but this will only come through engagement with your task. Look back to Chapter 5 for diagnostic exercises on test anxiety.

Illustration – Tug-of-war teams (visualising the scene)

The struggle experienced in an exam may seem as if a mental tug-of-war is going on. The negative team is on one side of the rope and each of the 'players' is shouting things such as 'you cannot do this', 'you are going to be a failure', 'you will not remember the facts' and 'you are going to make a fool of yourself'. On the other side is a group of 'players' that say things such as 'read the questions carefully', 'make a brief outline to get started', 'structure your responses', 'list names and dates', etc. It is as if you are standing in the middle of the two teams and must decide which one you are going to listen to and encourage. What you should do is blow the whistle on the negative players and demand silence from them. You can then speak to the positive players and instruct them to grasp the rope firmly with both hands, and then get into the rhythm of pulling at regular intervals. Gradually, your positive team can pull the rope over to their side in small steps until victory is secured.

8.5 Combining skills and resources

The resources you will need in an exam (apart from the practical things such as stationery) are the qualities you will carry inside you. In other words, the knowledge that you have accumulated, the understanding you have developed and the outline plans you have memorised. Once your mind has been activated, your resources will flow into your conscious mind. A driver does not need to sit and try to recall what all the instruments in the car are for every time he or she enters the vehicle. Neither do drivers need to think of every road sign or traffic signal that they may encounter on the journey. They just need to start the engine, press the accelerator, release the clutch, move through the gears, etc., and their automatic powers of coordination will work efficiently.

> *If you have done adequate preparation for your exams, then all that remains is to marshal and mobilise your resources in the test room.*

However, how you use the resources will be determined by the skills you have developed over time. Skills are learned by experience and practice, and the deployment of them will enable you to save time, focus on the task at hand, address the questions and structure your responses. The checklist that follows is designed to provide you with an outline of both the resources and skills that will enable you to function optimally in an exam. The various issues raised here have either been covered already or will be covered later in this book.

Checklist — Exam resources and skills

Resources

- ✓ Knowledge of relevant book chapters or sections
- ✓ Knowledge of relevant journal articles or abstracts
- ✓ Awareness of major topics in the field of study
- ✓ Retention of major contributors' names and concepts
- ✓ Knowledge of previous exam papers and questions
- ✓ Knowledge of outline plans and mnemonics
- ✓ Knowledge of pointers highlighted in lecture material

Skills

- ✓ Flexibility to 'tweak' outlines to the 'twist' in the question
- ✓ Ability to focus only on what is asked

✓ Facility to apply responses imaginatively
✓ Capacity to integrate information from a range of sources
✓ Aptitude at fitting subsections into appropriate time frames
✓ Capacity to provide clear evidence of independent learning
✓ Ability to focus on a critical rather than descriptive approach

8.6   Task and time management

In relation to task management, the first essential is to learn not 'to major on the minor'. If you get engrossed with minor issues, you will run out of the time you need to incorporate all the essentials. Time and task management are therefore integrated.

One myth that some students appear to believe is that if they are brilliant in one aspect of a topic this will compensate for inadequacies in another.

A little reflection will show you that fewer ideas will limit your ability to make the comparisons and contrasts needed to provide you with adequate material for a good critique.

Example — Task management

Question: What are the features that make blockbuster films popular?

Issues to cover:

- Film previews and reviews
- Popularity and profile of actors
- Time of year when released (e.g. before/after Christmas)
- Other similar films (saturation point)
- Anecdotal reports from patrons and/or friends
- Awards received (e.g. Oscars, BAFTAs)
- Trailers before other films
- Good plot/surprise aspects/special effects
- Size of budget
- Targeted audience (e.g. age group)

(Continued)

(Continued)

Your first goal in addressing a question should be to list the major points that you intend to cover. Once you begin to make your list, other points will occur to you. At this stage you cannot afford to be lengthy — all you need is a key word or two that will sum up and remind you of what you need to cover. After you have done that, you should then think of approximately how long you have to cover each point. Also, you should consider whether some points are more important than others. You may need to give the more important points extended treatment, or it may be sufficient to draw attention to the less important points in your conclusion. The example used above in task management will also be used below in time management.

Example — Time management

Imagine that the exam question above has been selected as one of two exam questions to be answered in a two-hour exam. You may decide on strategy principles such as those listed here:

- You have one hour to answer the question
- You have identified 10 main points you wish to address
- You have already used up 10 minutes reading the question and outlining the points
- Now there are 50 minutes left to complete the 10 points
- As insurance, in case you run out of time, you put an asterisk at some of the least important points that you can combine at the end in one paragraph
- Ten points over 50 minutes = 5 minutes per point (an approximation)
- You will also want to find a minute or two for opening and closing points
- Be flexible enough for some points that may be a little shorter or longer than others
- Get into this way of thinking well in advance of your test

Exercise — Time management on a past paper

To develop this skill, look at a past paper on a topic that you have yet to be tested on. Follow the procedures outlined above for time and task management. Divide your topic up into major headings and subheadings and allocate time accordingly. Allow some time for planning, structuring and the introduction and conclusion.

8.7 Targeting the questions

As noted in Chapter 1, what you must not do in academia is prolong indecision, and this is nowhere more applicable than in an exam. Indecision may sometimes be a problem for students who have worked hard and prepared widely – they are faced with the luxury of choice. If you enter a test room equipped to answer every question on the paper, you may have a completely different problem from students who 'question spot'. Given that their choice is so limited, it is easier for them to select their questions (if they are lucky enough to have any), and get started more quickly. However, it may be that the more conscientious students will have favoured topics that they will prefer to tackle. In general, therefore, it may not be a bad strategy to have preference questions, especially if you have a tendency to be indecisive. The points outlined below are designed to help you target questions in an exam as quickly and efficiently as possible. What you should try to avoid is to start on one question and then abandon this for another. When you draft an outline in your essay plan, you should know if you have adequate material and interest to tackle the question thoroughly.

Checklist – Strategy points for targeting a question

✓ Know before the exam what you are prepared to tackle
✓ Place an X at the questions you have ruled out
✓ Tick the questions you might be able to address
✓ Double tick the ones you finally select as your preferred option
✓ Select the order in which you wish to answer the questions and number accordingly
✓ It is sensible to take your best question first
✓ Write the question out fully before you commence (unless, for example, there is a long quote with it)
✓ If you cannot decide on your second question then suspend judgement until you finish the first (your confidence will grow with a good first essay)
✓ Commence your first outline and work out the approximate time for each point

You may prefer your own detailed strategic system to that presented above, but the important point is to take control and remain in control of the test situation. The advantage of placing ticks (or your own preferred notation) as codes alongside questions is that you will not waste time accidentally re-reading questions you have ruled out.

8.8 Drafting the templates

The template referred to here is a mental framework that enables you to organise and structure your learning material around an outline that will serve your memory, understanding and application to a question. However, it should not be forgotten that at university, examinations are not set to test your ability to hand back through an exam what you have been given verbatim in lectures. You should be able to demonstrate that you have read from a number of sources and been able to come to some conclusions based on the evidence you have accumulated. The template you have will provide a working structure that you will bring to the exam but you must be ready to adapt it to the orientation of the question.

Illustration — The plumber's role

When a plumber sets out to install a new plumbing system, he or she must have all the materials and tools that will be needed for the job. The plumber may need to measure, cut, thread, ream and bend the pipes in order to fit them to the walls and attach them to boxes. No two houses are likely to be exactly the same and the plumber must begin the work with a readiness to be adaptable. The tools and materials may remain the same from one house to the next, but the plumber must not, for example, bend the pipe under the assumption that the angle on a wall is identical to the one in the previous house.

And so it is with the exam. You may go into the test room armed with the same facts and figures as the students one year before (except that you have also updated the material by at least one year!). You must be ready, however, to change the order in which the facts should be presented, and perhaps the emphasis may need to change. For example, there may be a need for more applied emphasis or a necessity for comparing and contrasting, etc.

A worked example — Gardner's model of intelligence

Outline of points:

- Traditional IQ encapsulates verbal/mathematical–logical/spatial abilities
- Gardner also adds bodily/musical/interpersonal/intrapersonal

(Continued)

(Continued)

- Critics argue that these add personality and talents to the pure measure of IQ
- Gardner argues that all the aspects of IQ are independent of each other
- Critics argue that this is not consistent with the evidence for general intelligence
- Gardner argues that some strands of evidence suggest support for his approach
- Critics argue that the traditional structure of IQ has a solid support base
- Gardner argues that the traditional approach breeds elitism and inhibits the potential of disadvantaged children
- He also argues that ability should be judged by what is important within a given culture
- Critics argue that the traditional approach can allow for Gardner's points without a paradigm shift

---

If you have learned a template like this for your topic (again, with a word or two for each point as memory joggers), you will have a mixture of knowledge and information combined with an ability to critique your material. If the material is learned in the above fashion then it can be easily and quickly adapted to a variety of exam questions as in the following examples:

- **Does the recent evidence support Gardner's model of intelligence?**

- **Does the recent evidence support the traditional view of intelligence?**

- **Does Gardner's model of intelligence or the traditional view have most empirical support?**

- **Is there any substance in the arguments against Gardner's model of intelligence?**

- **Should the debate about Gardner's model of intelligence be resolved by hard empirical evidence or by an assessment of its usefulness in the educational system?**

- **What does the future hold for Gardner's model of intelligence?**

- **Is there justification for the popularity of Gardner's model of intelligence in some educational circles?**

You have got to have the flexibility to take the points you have prepared and work them around the question.

Some points will not be relevant at all and some will be more relevant than others. You may sometimes have to sacrifice or lay less emphasis on the points that interest you most.

8.9   A sketch plan

As an example of how you might prepare an outlined response to an exam question, consider the following. The question to be addressed is: 'Evaluate the causes and consequences of alcoholism'. Immediately, you can see you will first need to define alcoholism, and then list the causes and consequences of alcoholism. You might prefer to draw these out rather than list them.

Causes of alcoholism	Consequences of alcoholism
Bad life events (bereavement/unemployment)	Disruption – home and family
Peer pressure (initially social drinking)	Disruption – work
Modelling on others (e.g. advertisements)	Disruption – social life
Boredom (lack of purpose)	Dependency – on alcohol as a drug
Loneliness (rejection and isolation)	Depletion (finances, health)
Depression/mood (coping strategy)	Duration of problem (chronic)
Family history (genetic and social)	Denial – presenting control to others

8.10   Warding off intrusive thoughts (see also Chapter 5)

After you have prepared diligently for your test, the 'spoilers' (intrusive thoughts) may come to impair your performance. These can be thought of as the distracting thoughts that 'eat up' your time by diverting your attention from the task at hand. As was previously noted in Chapter 5, the distracting thoughts can be related to the exam or totally unconnected with it. Examples of the former are worrying what the assessor will think, how poorly you may be performing in relation to others or how inadequate your preparation has been. Examples of the latter are thoughts about current events in the media, plans for weekend activities or annoyance at some recent interaction with a friend. Whether these 'intruders' come in a pleasant or unpleasant guise does not matter in the final analysis – they have the same spoiling effect. But are there strategies that can be used to ward off intrusive thoughts? The list below has been designed to help you arm yourself against the 'enemy' in your exams.

Checklist — Exam strategy for controlling intrusive thoughts

- ✓ Be aware that they can happen to you
- ✓ Be persuaded that you need not let them control you
- ✓ If necessary, make a note in rough work — e.g. 'do not drift!'
- ✓ Prevent your thoughts drifting in the early stages of the exam
- ✓ Drafting outlines for the questions will help you keep focused
- ✓ Do not look around you for distractions
- ✓ Give irrelevant thoughts permission to return only after the test!
- ✓ Talking to yourself brings more control than listening to yourself!
- ✓ Remind yourself that you are only enclosed in the exam room for a very short period and can reward yourself with a preferred treat afterwards
- ✓ When distracted you can write key words in rough work to restore your focus on the task
- ✓ Re-read the last couple of paragraphs you have written to get you back on track
- ✓ Simply being aware of the problem is often more than half the battle

8.11 Strategies for questions

In this section there will be a worked example followed by a practice example for you to tackle. The examples will be quite general so that students from all backgrounds and subject areas will be able to tackle them. Moreover, in the practice example there will be questions to guide you through.

A worked example — Addressing an exam question (A)

Question: Critically discuss whether professional outdoor competitive sports games should be suspended during the heart of the winter.

Introduction ⎰ There are strongly opposing views
⎱ The subject comes up at regular intervals
New arguments are needed to avoid a stagnant debate

Arguments for winter breaks

Spectators cold
Pitches chopped up
Miserable journey home
   (cold, wet, dark)
Sports quality impaired (muddy pitches)
Summer sport not adequately tested
   before
Foreign players disadvantaged

Arguments against winter breaks

Spectators on holiday in summer
Protect pitches (heating, cover, roof)
Sport 'shortens' winter for many
Hard summer pitches cause injuries
Summer weather too hot for sport
Summer free for other activities

Conclusions ⎰ At least debate is healthy and should continue
Limited trial runs are inadequate
Change is risky (but might be worth it)
At least one model has been pioneered (Scottish soccer)
Issues involved include quality, convenience and enjoyment

You can decide whether to discuss point and counterpoint one by one, or to divide all points for, followed by all points against (or vice versa). The advantage of the former strategy is that if you run out of time you will at have thrashed out both sides of at least some aspects of the argument.

Addressing an exam question (B) — A practice example

Question: Should students take a year out to travel after graduation?

Introduction: Perhaps a few remarks about the popularity of the practice, and a kind of hidden pressure to do this for fear that you may 'miss the boat'.

(Continued)

(Continued)

You may prefer to list your own points for and against. Or, if you need help to get your mind activated, the following list of issues may help to give you some cues. For example, you can also look at the opposite of each of these points.

- Need for a break after a hard study programme
- It's now or never?
- Finances — affordable?
- Broadening experience
- Immediate job opportunities ruined?
- Cementing friendships with others?
- Later regret at missing the opportunity to travel?
- Once working, no turning back for prolonged travel?
- What will prospective employers think?
- Safety and health issues?

Conclusion: Each individual must decide and circumstances may differ from student to student. You may be broadly in favour of the idea, but the opportunity must be wisely used. For some, it may be better to wait, and short, frequent breaks are a reasonable alternative.

Checklist — The mechanics of an exam

- ✓ Look after the preliminaries and the practicalities
- ✓ Ensure that you have noted the time, venue, etc., correctly
- ✓ Prepare travel arrangements for the event
- ✓ Bring all necessary stationery
- ✓ Find your allocated place in the test room in good time
- ✓ Carry revision outline notes for the journey
- ✓ 'Carry' your revision notes in your memory
- ✓ Bring a watch for planning your time
- ✓ Bring liquid if you have a tendency to dry up

Checklist — The dynamics of an exam

- ✓ Choose the questions efficiently
- ✓ Organise your time economically

✓ Design your outlines effectively
✓ Begin to write enthusiastically
✓ Remain focused on your task exclusively

SUMMARY

Chapter 8 summary points:

➢ Adapt a positive mindset towards exams

➢ Keep panic at bay by attending to practical exam issues

➢ Prepare your resources and use your skills

➢ Be ready to target the questions you will address

➢ Prepare to take control of time management

➢ Prepare to organise your division of labour (task management)

➢ Be ready to turn stressful reactions to your advantage

➢ 'Tweak' your memorised outlines to the 'twist' in the question

9 What Examiners Look For

9.1 Answering the set question!

It is wise to remember that it is possible to look without seeing – we can sometimes be primed to see what we want to see rather than what is actually there. Of course if you are asked to write an appreciation of a piece of art or poetry it may well be that you should project your personal interpretation on to the work. Outside this, it is more likely that you will be expected to produce relevant evidence and arguments to address the set question in the exam with a clear focus. Although the virtue of using past papers for revision has been extolled, the danger with this approach is that you may twist the meaning of a question into what you hope it is going to be. Another danger is that the question you wanted so much is right in front of your eyes but you fail to see it because the form of wording is different from the previous occasions and in blind panic you de-select that one as an option!

Therefore, the general advice at this point is, slow down, read carefully and make your question selection advisedly.

When you have made your choice, write the question out and this will be the final insurance that you have not misunderstood its intent.

In a famous optical illusion, Rubin's vase can be seen as a vase or as two faces that look towards each other. You can see it both ways and it can 'change' from one to the other. In contrast, exam questions are usually set so that they can be addressed in one way (although there is room for variety in structure, style and perhaps some substance).

A worked example

Question: Evaluate the important ingredients in the security, prosperity and happiness of a city.

Strategy for response: First, make a list of major city functions, such as:

Health	Infrastructure	Crime
Education	Housing/Property	Entertainment
Transport	Finance/Banking	Leisure/Sport
Trade	Parks and Greens	Art/Museums
Security	Traffic	Employment

What you should not do is:

- Merely describe the function of each
- Focus only on the ones that are of interest to you
- Go off on a tangent such as the effects of flooding on a city

What you might think of doing is:

- Describe each one in a brief sentence of two
- Highlight how the quality of life would be diminished if any of the above were missing
- Show that the various facets are dependent on other aspects of city life
- You may want to list essential and non-essential services and then rank each of these in turn

9.2 Initial evidence of focus

It is said that 'you never get a second chance to make a first impression', and in the first paragraph of your response to the exam question you have the opportunity to shape the initial impression in the examiner's mind. That does not mean that his or her final impression is sealed, but it does give you the opportunity to set up and then confirm a positive overall impression. If the initial few sentences are good in quality, this will also help you to settle down and you will feel spurred on to do well.

PRACTICAL SCENARIO: A JOB INTERVIEW

To give a good initial impression when you go for a job interview, you could:

- **Walk confidently into the room**

- **Be smartly and neatly dressed, trimmed and clean**

- **Smile and say hello to each member of the interview panel**

- **Briefly get eye contact with each panel member but without a fixed gaze**

- **Shake hands if offered and exchange courtesies diplomatically**

- **Sit when you are invited to**

In an exam situation you do not have the non-verbal cues that you can use to create a good impression in an interview, but you have written cues you can use to demonstrate that you have purpose, focus, direction, knowledge and understanding. In the next section you will see how rough work can be used in shaping a good impression, but another tool is the preliminary use of key words and terms.

A worked example

Question: Discuss the essential elements that help in building good friendships that will last.

(Continued)

(Continued)

A good strategy is to list the important ideas that spring to mind, such as:

- Not being too demanding
- Inviting your friends to events that are important to you
- Overlooking faults
- Showing acts of kindness and generosity
- Being willing listen when friends need someone to talk to

You may want to add a few of your own to the above list.

It is also a good strategy to drop key words such as these into the opening sentences to demonstrate that you know exactly where you are taking the examiner in your journey together. As an example of mapping out a strategy in advance, think of going for a walk in a country forest park – you may find maps at the beginning of the walk so that you can decide which routes you want to take and in what order.

In the first couple of sentences of your exam question response you can, as it were, create a map for your examiner. You can tell her or him where you are going to take them. Be sure to give the impression that you know where you are leading them.

9.3   Rough work may be helpful

Some students prefer to use mind maps in drawing up plans for an essay or exam question. It is acceptable to draw out your own mind map design, and this is all you will be able to do if you opt for this method in your exams as you cannot resort to software. However, this approach may not be appealing to all and you may prefer to use a simple structure approach such as the use of headings and subheadings. When mind mapping is used with software packages you can achieve complexity by using colour codes, circles, squares, rectangles and ellipses, and you can set up pathways in which your variables are joined by direct or indirect routes. These may be very useful in your revision or even in a presentation, but in your exam you will not need all the decorative niceties. Your aim should be to draw a basic map as quickly as possible. The more complex your map is, the more difficult it will be to remember all the points and the longer it will take to draw out all the parts. Consider the following question and then see how the response can be briefly plotted out in a mind map (or even in the form of a flow chart).

Question: Outline the essential factors and applications of communication in a variety of human settings.

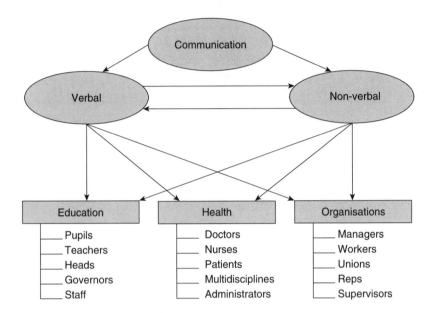

9.4 Balance, connection and fluency

On the point of balance, it is essential that you do justice to all aspects of an argu-ment. For example, in terms of length, this suggests that paragraphs should be of approximately similar length although there are no hard-and-fast rules. Some aspects of your subject may require a little more treatment than others, but if you alter-nate between very long and very short paragraphs your argument may appear to be lopsided.

It is also vital that you do not suddenly introduce an argument that appears to be grossly out of place or sequence – there has to be some connection between your points and you should not assume that your reader will always see these without you demonstrating them.

Finally, aim to communicate the impression that your work flows from start to finish. If you achieve this, you will have integrated a variety of valid points into one coherent and convincing whole. What fluency will do for you is to give your essay some life. Your response to the question should not be a mere list of hard, cold facts that are joined up by nothing more than punctuation and conjunctions.

Use of illustrations and applications can add colour, spice and variety to your responses unless these have been outlawed in your subject domain. However, illustrations should not become an end in themselves, and neither should they be irrelevant or forced.

A worked example

Question: What are the advantages and disadvantages of the widespread introduction of computers into higher education?

- An additional task that almost all students are now required to master
- Possible advantage to those from comfortable backgrounds
- Most universities are well equipped with modern computers
- Pressure on finding computer space at busy times in university libraries
- Students can still schedule time for off-peak periods
- Up-to-date electronic journals are readily available
- Library searches are much easier than before
- Word processing means work is easily modified
- Quality of presentations can be enhanced using computer graphics
- Advantages include spelling and grammar checks and word counts
- Anxious students avoid using computers and may therefore fall behind
- Economically disadvantaged students may not be put on an equal footing
- Computer skills are transferable (across modules and years)
- Computer skills are impressive on a CV
- Computers can become addictive – a time-wasting distraction for students

This is an applied topic and all students will have views on it both from their own personal experience and from observation of other students. If this were your exam topic, you could go into the test armed with information from computer and educational studies, and this could be complemented by case studies and your own anecdotal experience and observations.

Exercise – See if you can condense each of the bullet points above into a brief word or two that you can use as memory joggers for your rough work in an exam. It may help to underline a key word or two in each. For example, just the use of 'CV' could help you remember the penultimate point.

Checklist – Golden Rules

- ✓ Can't say everything about everything
- ✓ Must make selections
- ✓ Choose examples from each domain
- ✓ Find some major headings
- ✓ Cluster examples under appropriate headings
- ✓ Draw connections between major concepts
- ✓ Decide on order for working through these step by step
- ✓ Decide if there is one or more central concept
- ✓ Avoid too much complexity in sketching outline
- ✓ Balance the number of issues under each heading

9.5   Corroborate with evidence

Many academic subjects are driven by theory, research and empirical findings, and if this is the case, then you must show that you know the relevant literature. The more evidence you can use the better (if you use it effectively). However, you cannot go into a detailed description of every relevant study you have read. Rather, you can summarise and show the relevance of a given study in a brief few sentences.

Make sure you give the impression that you are using the evidence to support your arguments and to build up your case.

Of course, you will want to come to some definitive conclusions in your exam essay, but on the journey there you will need to show that you have reached your conclusions in the light of (perhaps) conflicting evidence. It may be that your overall conclusion is that the balance of probability lies in one side of the argument, but you may conclude that further studies are needed to address some unresolved issues. An example of a question like this would be the MMR issue that was discussed in Chapter 7: Can it be concluded with certainty that the triple vaccine for mumps, measles and rubella is now safe?

Checklist — Using evidence

✓ Describe findings accurately and succinctly
✓ Use relevant names (authors of theories or research)
✓ Use as many dates as you can remember
✓ Cover the development of the topic and incorporate up-to-date findings
✓ Present all sides of an argument
✓ Only make strong claims that are evidence-based
✓ Use a variety of evidence to build a case (showing convergence)
✓ Come to conclusions based on the balance of probabilities (if need be)
✓ Identify unresolved or inconclusive issues
✓ Map out where future research needs to go

9.6   Independent and problem-based learning

What your assessors will not be looking for is a verbatim account of what they delivered to you in a lecture or tutorial. You should show evidence that you have read from the sources they have directed you to in reading lists. Examiners also like to see that you have taken some initiative by delving into other sources that they had not highlighted.

> From the standpoint of a marker, it is most refreshing to assess students who have taken the time and trouble to bring some new facet of research to the subject under investigation.

It is especially impressive if students can integrate some up-to-date sources, and this should not be too difficult given the plethora of electronic journals that are available in modern universities. Moreover, these sources are a great advantage when there are constraints upon your time. They are easily accessed and summaries of central findings are often available in abstract form. The main findings can be rapidly outlined, grasped and noted.

A form of learning that has been advocated in higher education circles and has gained popularity is the notion of problem-based learning. In this form of learning activity, a group of students is given a task by their tutor, and individual students go their separate ways to extract the information they need. When each has finished their task they come together and use their collated information to try to solve the problem that had been posed by the tutor. Instead of being taught directly, students endeavour to find answers for themselves, and it is believed that this can be an effective form of learning because it facilitates a deeper processing of information. Therefore, in order to prepare thoroughly for your exams, you may want to engage in some problem-solving activities either alone or with other students.

DIRECTIONS FOR PROBLEM-BASED LEARNING

- Find a question or problem that will get you engaged with your topic

- Trace relevant sources and read around the topic

- Make a full list of all the relevant ideas

- Rank in order the steps that will lead to the solution

- Draw these out in a mental map or a flow chart

- Judge if any step can be removed without making a difference

- Is there more than one route to your goal?

- Are there direct and indirect pathways that should be mapped out?

- Are there bi-directional pathways?

- Is there one answer or multifaceted answers?

These steps will become clearer after you look at the worked example and the diagram presented below.

A worked example – Low birth weight babies:
what is the cause?

- Smoking in pregnant women has been implicated as a possible cause
- Stress has also been highlighted
- Stressful women might be more likely to smoke during pregnancy
- The father's smoking habits have also been suggested
- Therefore stress in fathers may also be implicated
- Parents can either buffer or trigger stress in each other
- Poor nutrition may also have a large causal impact
- Both parents may be responsible for the mother's poor nutrition
- A genetic component might be implicated, and also inactivity
- A conceptual diagram can be drawn to suggest possible causal pathways

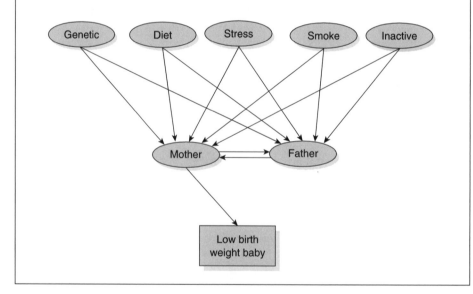

Like so many problems, there is a multifaceted explanation and by presenting the problem in diagram form you will show the examiner that you are aware of all the direct, indirect and bi-directional effects. For example, the mother and father may both influence low birth weight babies through genetics. They may also influence each other through four of the five variables shown in the diagram. It is clear that to put the whole problem down to pregnant women smoking is rather naïve.

Exercise – If you look at the five variables at the top of the diagram you may be able to work out how some of them impact on each other, and you can draw linking lines with arrows to denote the pathways.

9.7   Characterised by critical thinking

It is possible to argue through issues in the world of academia without becoming vitriolic towards other colleagues or fellow researchers. Critical thinking goes on all the time and academics constantly raise questions and problems in relation to each other's work. It is a violation of academic professionalism to run a vendetta against a colleague. Students sometimes find it a little difficult to make the transition from the secure world of comfortable thought and certainty to the real world of academia where findings evolve and develop through critical thinking, which may sometimes appear to be more like verbal sparring.

> *You should understand clearly that it is critical thinking that will get you your best grades in your exams, but the critical thinking must be evidence-based and not driven by personal prejudices or hunches.*

It is often a difficult task to rise above our personal, subjective world in order to evaluate objectively the full range of evidence without giving the impression that we have a personal 'axe to grind'. A writer can set up the alternatives to their preferred explanations to knock them down again in order to give the impression that they are even-handed and objective. Emotional involvement with a given topic may not be a bad thing in driving the investigation but it can lead to disguised distortions of reality. In order to illustrate critical thinking with an example, we will therefore address the issue of prejudice.

A worked example – Critical thinking about prejudice

Imagine that you have been asked the following question in an exam:
Discuss the assertion that it is impossible for a human being to be totally free from prejudice. Before examining the drafted response below, you might want to make some notes of your own in response.

(Continued)

(Continued)

It may help to start with a definition of prejudice: A prejudiced person can be defined as being like a jury that gives a verdict before it hears all the evidence.

- All grown-up human beings are likely to have or have had some degree of prejudice against others
- Prejudiced people attend to and select information that confirms their views
- Prejudiced people are likely to filter out information that does not support their views, or they will absorb it as an exception that proves the rule
- Prejudice is very resistant to change
- Prejudice may be intransigent because it is perceived as a mechanism for preservation and a buffer against insecurity
- Many will not admit to prejudice unless they are with trusted friends
- Some may not even realise that they are prejudiced
- Many may like to present the façade of fairness and objectivity
- The middle classes may be more cunning in their use of prejudice
- These complexities may make prejudice more difficult to address
- Getting to know the people you are prejudiced against may help to reduce prejudice
- Working models that have attempted to counteract prejudice is a useful starting point
- Courageous individuals who admit their prejudices (and the wrongness of them) may be more effective challenging others than those who merely point the accusing finger
- The goal of eliminating prejudice entirely may be unrealistic
- It may be possible to reduce prejudice and bring it under control

A glance at the above points will clearly demonstrate that you are armed with a series of points and counterpoints that will form the heart of a good, critical essay.

9.8 Year one and beyond

If you are in the first year of a university course it is likely that your results will not count towards your final degree classification. Therefore, all that will be required is to pass your exams at the stipulated level (typically 40 per cent in the UK for undergraduate programmes). That does not mean that you should content yourself with marginal passes, as this is not good for your confidence or anxiety! However, the knowledge that your degree classification is not at stake will give you the time and opportunities to develop the skills presented and advocated in this book. If you have already progressed beyond year one, then it is essential that you cultivate the skills presented in this book. The object of learning is not just about reproducing knowledge and demonstrating good memory skills. It is also about:

- **Addressing the question directly**

- **Writing succinctly and with focus**

- **Using a critical thinking approach**

- **Using relevant and up-to-date evidence to support your claims**

- **Presenting balanced arguments**

If what you have been doing to date has not been working for you in terms of the grades you are attaining, then it is time to do some diagnostic troubleshooting.

Do not allow yourself to lapse into the thinking mode where you convince yourself that you cannot change. It is possible to change your thinking style and strategy into one that will produce dividends for you. The following summary checklist will also help you to focus your attention on your strengths and weaknesses.

Checklist – What examiners look for

✓ Ensure that you are addressing the question before you start writing
✓ A mind map or flow chart, or headings and subheadings, will aid your essay structure and help you plan and pace your answer
✓ Aim for a balanced structure that avoids padding and does justice to all facets of an argument
✓ Hit all the right notes in your introductory paragraph and include relevant key words
✓ Make a point of sprinkling your exam essay liberally with cited evidence
✓ It is useful to demonstrate that you have done some independent learning
✓ Evidence of critical thinking will demonstrate that you have learned at a deeper level than rote reproduction

✓ Problem-based learning will provide you with an impressive format for addressing exam issues

✓ Time management (highlighted in earlier chapters) will allow you to pace out all the issues you aim to tackle

9.9   The key words in the question

IF YOU ARE ASKED TO WRITE A DISCUSSION

Whenever you are engaged in discussion, you are *examining* possibilities and *exploring* various avenues of thought. There should be a tone of investigation and enquiry, but with the important proviso that there is an end product. The discussion should be going somewhere – it must have shape and direction. There is room for a discussion to be tentative, but no place for it to be vague.

As an example, you could think of a television discussion show that includes a panel of experts and a person in the chair to guide the proceedings. If you are the person in the chair you would be concerned to:

• **Establish that the invited guests represent all shades of opinion on the issue**

• **Ensure that contributors have the opportunity to articulate their views**

• **Give contributors the opportunity to respond when their views are challenged**

• **Prevent any individual monopolising the discussion**

• **Control the interruptions that would make the discussion chaotic**

• **Summarise the conclusions in a fair and even-handed manner**

In an exam you are to be 'the chairperson' and it will be your responsibility to conduct the discussion in a well-ordered, fair and thorough manner. Although the tone of the discussion is different from, say, a critique, this does not mean that it should be tame in nature. There is room in the discussion for a vigorous exploration of evidence and counter arguments.

IF YOU ARE ASKED TO WRITE A CRITICAL REVIEW

The tone of a critique should be a little more 'adversarial' than a discussion.

In the discussion you are the chair to guide the panel, but in the critique you are the judge to guide the court proceedings.

Imagine there is a defence team and a prosecution team, and your aim is to find the evidence that will stand up in a court of law. You should not be afraid to 'chop down' claims that do not stand up in the light of the evidence. However, that does not mean (to change the metaphor) that you should be a 'knife-happy' surgeon who is intent on operating on every condition. Do not criticise just for the sake of it, or give the impression that you have been 'baptised in lemon juice!' What you really need to ascertain through your critique is what is left of the issue or claim when you hold it up to test it against the evidence? If the basic premise has been supported with evidence again and again, then you can argue that the evidence is robust. For example, you can pose questions, such as those presented below:

- Has the claim, hypothesis or theory stood the test of time?

- Are large claims made on the basis of very flimsy evidence?

- Do various studies leave an impression of uncertainty and a need for further investigation?

- Does it appear that aspects of previous investigation have been driven by prejudice or vested interests?

- Is the evidence supporting the results weak, moderate or strong?

- Should you end by highlighting certainties and uncertainties?

- Can you identify issues that are no longer relevant to the debate (red herrings)?

- Can you earmark issues for further investigation?

- Are there issues that are going in the expected direction and are clearly promising?

Exercise – If you wish, use these questions to challenge the issues raised in the MMR example in Chapter 7.

Exercise – Write your own checklist on the essential steps in a critique (think of yourself as a judge in court presiding over the prosecution and defence lawyers). The exercise will be easier if you choose a theme such as 'Should parents be allowed to smack their children?'

✓ ....

✓ ....

✓ ....

✓ ....

✓ ....

IF YOU ARE ASKED TO COMPARE AND CONTRAST

If you are asked in an exam or course work essay to compare and contrast two concepts, you will need to identify a range of issues that you can discuss within this context. You may begin by making a list of all the things that the two concepts have in common, and then list all the factors in which they differ. It is best to identify an equal number of issues (if possible) under each heading so that the conclusions are balanced.

A worked example – Compare and contrast popular and classical music

Similarities	Differences
Both use the same music clefs	Pop often associated with teenagers
Wide range of instruments used	Pop often linked to lively parties and discos

(Continued)

(Continued)

Performed with or without lyrics	Pop may be louder and more shocking
Live and recorded performances	Classical often preferred by the middle classes
Listened to for pleasure, relaxation, inspiration and mood control	Classical often has a more complex structure
	Classical pieces are of longer duration
Variety of styles	Classical pieces often have more musicians
Both used in films and advertisements	Different conventions for dress

In drawing this to a conclusion, you could say that:

- Some people listen to both
- Some listen exclusively to one or the other
- Performers have 'migrated' from one to the other
- Some writers/composers have integrated both
- Both serve the needs of individuals and crowds
- Both have useful applications to advertisements, films, therapy, etc.

Exercise – Write your own summary checklist on the major factors involved in producing a well-rounded essay that compares and contrasts two issues.

✓ ....

✓ ....

✓ ....

✓ ....

✓ ....

Another variation of the comparing and contrasting approach is when you are asked to outline the advantages and disadvantages of an issue (see the worked example on the advantages and disadvantages of the widespread introduction of computers in higher education in section 9.4 above). You may want to look back at this example to see if you can classify the advantages and disadvantages and add any points that are needed to balance the arguments. Alternatively, examine the advantages and disadvantages of small, street-corner stores and large supermarkets, or think up a new example of your own.

IF YOU ARE ASKED TO EVALUATE

Illustration – Antique objects and antiquated concepts

If an expert were asked to value a painting or a piece of sculpture, she would be keen to ascertain who the artist was and when the artwork was created. There is no doubt that some objects increase in value with the passage of time. If objects have stood the test of time, they may be very valuable, especially if they were painted or constructed by a master craftsperson.

And yet, in academia, the opposite can be true. Although a concept or theory may have been popular and widely accepted 30 years ago, more recent research findings may have chipped away at the foundations over the decades. Other aspects may now have been added to the original proposition, so that what is left now is a modified version of the original. Therefore, if you are asked to evaluate, you may want to consider the following:

- **State the basic premise**

- **Show where findings have attacked aspects of this premise**

- **Highlight aspects that have been strong enough to endure**

- **Identify any new aspects that have been added to the original**

- Present the 'new animal' with its additions and subtractions

- Demonstrate the usefulness of the concept

- Map out the reasons why the premise is set to persist in the future

To wrap up this section just read over the following points. The italicised words are the key words in exam questions. This will give you an idea of how examine questions can be 'spun' from various angles. Remember, each key word requires a different kind of approach.

- *Evaluate* whether modern prisons achieve the aims of reducing crime and reforming criminals.

- *Discuss* other factors that might be run in parallel with the prison system that would be a positive complement to its work.

- *Compare* and *contrast* the work of prisons with rehabilitation day centres.

- Write a *critique* on whether there is value in exploring the criminal mind.

9.10 Attention to the qualifying words in a question

EXAMPLE 1 – IF YOU ARE ASKED TO ADDRESS MORE THAN ONE ISSUE

A close inspection of an exam question may reveal that you are required to address more than one central issue. Unless you have been guided otherwise, you should, in general, try to give equal weighting to all the issues. Consider how you would address the following question: 'Why are some students prone to catch colds, and can anything be done to address this problem?'

The second part of the question should be as important as the first and clearly requires more than a 'yes' or 'no' answer. In the example provided here, you would be advised to link each potential cause with a corresponding prevention or cure. It is probable that examiners will award 50 per cent for each part of the question.

EXAMPLE 2 — WHEN A FEW WORDS FILTER THE DIRECTION OF THE QUESTION

Some questions may direct you into a line of response in the last few words (or in the opening words). Therefore, read the question carefully so that you do not go off track. Consider the following question: 'Discuss the impact of airport noise on those that live near airports.'

The last part of the question excludes:

- Those who work at airports

- Those who work and travel on planes

- Those who travel to and from airports

- Those who live in low fly zones away from airports

However, it includes the effects of noise:

- During the daytime

- During the nighttime

- On health, quality of life, etc.

- In airports generally — no one airport is specified

- On the value of houses in the vicinity

The question does not specify how close to the airports people should be living in order to be taken into account in your essay — it could be one, two or five miles. So you are probably expected to address the issue in general without specifying a distance.

EXAMPLE 3 — WHEN THE QUESTION DOES NOT HAVE A 'KEY' WORD

Another issue to bear in mind is that you may not be asked *directly* to write a critique, discussion or evaluation, but your tutors will probably have directed you to use a critical approach in general in approaching all exam questions. Take the following two examples:

'Should sex education be given to children in primary education?'

'Should Shakespeare's plays be left in their original Elizabethan language?'

Although no key words such as 'discuss' or 'evaluate' are used here, it is evident that the questions have been designed to elicit an essay that includes points and counterpoints.

EXAMPLE 4 — WHEN THE QUESTION LEAVES THE SCOPE OPEN-ENDED

Sometimes examiners will leave you to select issues to illustrate the broader principles in the question. This type of essay needs careful thought in order to find the correct balance between the inclusion of too much or too little material. Given that we covered motivation in an earlier chapter, we will use this as our example: 'Discuss with the use of examples the assertion that motivation is the dynamic behind human change.'

You could select examples on:

• **Attraction and reproduction**

• **Power and promotion**

• **Earnings and savings**

• **Aggression and control**

• **Status and education**

The problem in the question is that you are not asked to discuss a specific number of issues. Rather, you must decide how many examples to include. To help you think through this issue, have a go at the following exercise.

Exercise – Suggest some problems that may be associated with: The use of (a) too few examples and (b) too many examples in your exam responses. Some suggestions are provided after this exercise if you need to consult them.

(a) Potential problems with too few examples in exam responses:

....

....

....

(b) Potential problems with too many examples in exam responses:

....

....

....

(a)   Potential problems with too few examples in exam responses

• **Temptation to be too descriptive**

• **Insufficient material to make adequate critical comparisons**

• **Extending material to fill space**

• **It may look as though you have not read widely enough**

(b)   Potential problems with too many examples in exam responses

• **It can read like a list and therefore distort essay form**

• **It may look like a memory exercise**

• **The common thread between examples may not be clear**

• **It could appear as a shallow exercise**

Exercise — Write your own checklist of the factors that you would choose to guide you in deciding how many examples you would use in responding to an exam question (i.e. if the number of examples to use is not specified).

✓ ....

✓ ....

✓ ....

✓ ....

✓ ....

SUMMARY

Chapter 9 summary points:

➢ Ensure you answer the question that has been set

➢ Avoid rough work that takes up too much time

➢ Present an introduction that shows focus and direction

➢ Provide balanced arguments that demonstrate objectivity

➢ Reinforce your arguments with references to evidence

➢ Ensure your responses are more critical than descriptive

➢ Show some evidence of independent learning

➢ Build your answer around the key words in the question

Appendix

The following measure was adapted from a questionnaire developed by Lees, author of *How To Get A Job You'll Love* (2001), and was modified for use in his work with students. It is not intended to be a rigorous psychometric test, but provides a few 'tasters' to give you a flavour of the range of abilities and talents that may contribute to the quality of your academic and personal life. Ring the yes/no answer that applies to you.

Cluster 1

I enjoy the challenge of crosswords or word games	Yes / No
Reading is usually a pleasurable experience for me	Yes / No
I like the opportunity to tell stories	Yes / No
I enjoy finding the right word to use	Yes / No

Cluster 2

I like to take most opportunities to practise mental arithmetic	Yes / No
I am good at solving mental arithmetic problems	Yes / No
My decisions are usually based on solid reasons rather than intuition	Yes / No
I come to decisions after searching out all sides of an argument	Yes / No

Cluster 3

I really enjoy drawing or sketching or painting a picture	Yes / No
I have a fine-tuned sense of direction	Yes / No

| I would enjoy the challenge of reverse-parking a car | Yes / No |
| I am quick and efficient at packing materials into a confined space | Yes / No |

Cluster 4

I like to keep my hands engaged with practical activities	Yes / No
I like the challenge of assembling things (e.g. furniture, models, etc.)	Yes / No
I enjoy hobbies requiring practical skills (e.g. carpentry, knitting, gardening)	Yes / No
I relish the opportunity to engage in sports activities	Yes / No

Cluster 5

I can easily reproduce the musical sounds I hear	Yes / No
I play at least one musical instrument regularly	Yes / No
I enjoy reading or listening to rhymes or poetry	Yes / No
I enjoy composing my own music or poems	Yes / No

Cluster 6

I enjoy opportunities to meet new people	Yes / No
I have a reputation for being a good listener	Yes / No
I have a good capacity to read the moods of others	Yes / No
I am good at communicating my feelings to others	Yes / No
I am quite skilled at handling interpersonal conflict	Yes / No

Cluster 7

| I allow my intuition to be my strongest guide | Yes / No |
| I only conform when this is consistent with my beliefs | Yes / No |

If I had a choice, I would prefer to be my own boss	Yes / No
I like to document regularly my personal thoughts and feelings	Yes / No

The above clusters represent Gardner's seven intelligences in the following order:

1 = Verbal/linguistic
2 = Logical/mathematical
3 = Visual/spatial
4 = Bodily/kinaesthetic
5 = Musical
6 = Interpersonal
7 = Intrapersonal (i.e. self-knowledge)

Scoring

Remember that these may not represent your actual ability in these domains, but your perception of your abilities. Also, the measures above take into account your interest in the specific area. It is possible that you may have considerable ability in one specific area but little interest in it, or considerable interest but limited ability.

CLUSTER 1 (VERBAL/LINGUISTIC)

If you responded 'yes' to any of the four items, this implies that you have a positive perception and interest in tasks associated with verbal and linguistic activities.

CLUSTER 2 (LOGICAL/MATHEMATICAL)

A 'yes' to the first two items shows an inclination to mathematical tasks, and a 'yes' to the next two items implies a tendency to practise and enjoy solving logical problems.

CLUSTER 3 (VISUAL/SPATIAL)

If you responded 'yes' to the first item, then you clearly enjoy visual tasks, and if your response was 'yes' to the next three items, you have a capacity to engage in spatial tasks.

CLUSTER 4 (BODILY/KINAESTHETIC)

'Yes' answers to the items in cluster 4 suggest that you are a very practical person who enjoys and is good at hand tasks. Obviously, the more items you circled 'yes', the more extensive this tendency is.

CLUSTER 5 (MUSICAL)

Positive responses to these items suggest that you have musical or poetic inclinations. Of course it clear that you do not need to have great ability to enjoy these activities. However, you can still put them to good use – in choosing the appropriate music for entertaining, creating a certain mood, etc.

CLUSTER 6 (INTERPERSONAL)

'Yes' answers to the five items in this cluster suggest that you have very good social and communication skills.

CLUSTER 7 (INTRAPERSONAL)

A positive response to these items implies that you have good self-knowledge and can put this to good use in dealing with your own moods, emotions and reactions. They also suggest that you can be quite independent when you need to be.

Some authors have argued against Gardner's approach and claim that it does not have sufficient evidence to support it and that it really merges intelligence with other factors, such as talents and personality (for example, see Eysenck, 1994). Nevertheless, it has become popular in educational circles because it allows teachers to value, encourage and develop children who have gifts that may not be nurtured within the traditional system. In addition, it can be argued that personality features and personal qualities will enable individuals to put their gifts to the best possible use. For example, you may be a very able individual who underachieves through lack of discipline, motivation, endurance and resilience. Also, you may not function efficiently in your work environment if you have not developed interpersonal, communication and social skills. Furthermore, if you can control your mood and fuel your motivation this can help assist the cultivation of your abilities.

References

Alpert, R. & Haber, N. (1960). Anxiety in academic achievement situations. *Journal of Abnormal and Social Psychology*, **61**(2): 207–15.

Aronson, E., Wilson, T.D. & Akert, R.M. (1994). *Social Sychology: The Heart and the Mind*. New York: HarperCollins College Publishers.

Bandura, A. (1986). *Social Foundations of Thought and Action: A Social Cognitive Theory*. Englewood Cliffs, NJ: Prentice-Hall.

Bandura, A. (1997). *Self-efficacy: The Exercise of Control*. New York: W.H. Freeman & Co.

Biggs, J. (1999). *Teaching for Quality Learning at University*. Buckingham: SRHE.

Cooper, C. (1999). *Intelligence and Abilities*. Hove, UK: Psychology Press Ltd.

Covington, M.V. & Omelich, C.L. (1987). 'I knew it cold before the exam': a test of the anxiety blockage hypothesis. *Journal of Educational Psychology*, **79**(4): 393–400.

Csikszentmihalyi, M. (1975). *Beyond Boredom and Anxiety*. San Francisco, CA: Jossey-Bass.

Deffenbacher, J.L. (1980). Worry and emotionality in test anxiety. In I.G. Sarason (ed.), *Test Anxiety: Theory, Research and Applications*. Hillside, NJ: LEA, pp. 111–24.

El-Zahhar, N.E. & Hocever, D. (1991). Cultural and sexual differences in test anxiety, trait anxiety and arousability. *Journal of Cross Cultural Psychology*, **22**(2): 238–49.

Elliot, E.S. & Dweck, C.S. (1988). Goals: an approach to motivation and achievement. *Journal of Personality and Social Psychology*, **54**: 5–12.

Eysenck, H.J. (1995). Trait theories of personality. In S.E. Hampson & A.M. Coleman (eds), *Individual Differences and Personality*. London: Longman.

Eysenck, M.W. (1994). *Individual Differences: Normal and Abnormal*. Hove, UK: Psychology Press Ltd.

Ganzer, V.J. (1968). Effects of audience presence and test anxiety on learning and retention in a serial learning situation. *Journal of Personality and Social Psychology*, **8**: 194–9.

Gardner, H. (1983). *Frames of Mind: The Theory of Multiple Intelligences*. New York: Basic Books.

Gecas, V. (1989). The social psychology of self-efficacy. *Annual Review of Sociology*, **15**: 291–316.

Gibbs, G. (1992). *Improving the Quality of Student Learning*. Bristol: Technical and Educational Services.

Goud, N. & Arkoff, A. (2003). *Psychology and Personal Growth* (6th edition). New York: Pearson Education.

Hayes, N. & Orrell, S. (1994). *Psychology: An Introduction*. London: Longman.

Hembree, R. (1988). Correlates, causes, effects and treatment of test anxiety. *Review of Educational Research*, **58**(1): 47–77.

Lees, J. (2001). *How To Get a Job You'll Love*. London: McGraw-Hill.

Lepper, M.R. & Greene, D. (eds) (1978). *The Hidden Costs of Reward*. Hillside, NJ: Erlbaum.

Liebert, R.M. & Morris, L.W. (1967). Cognitive and emotional components of test anxiety: a distinction and some initial data. *Psychological Reports*, **20**: 975–8.

Luchins, A.S. (1942). Mechanisms in problem solving: the effects of *Einstellung*. *Psychological Monographs*, **54**(248).

McIlroy, D. (2003). *Studying at University: How To Be a Successful Student*. London: Sage.

McIlroy, D., Bunting, B. & Adamson, G. (2000). An evaluation of the factor structure and predictive utility of a test anxiety scale with reference to students' past performance and personality indices. *British Journal of Educational Psychology*, **70**: 17–32.

Millar, G.A. (1956). The magic number seven, plus or minus two: some limits in our capacity for processing information. *Psychological Review*, **63**: 81–93.

Prosser, A. (1995). Doing something about student motivation. *Hersda News*, **17**(2): 8–10.

Ramsden, P. (1992). *Learning to Teach in Higher Education*. London and New York: Routledge.

Ryan, R.M. & Deci, E.L. (2000). Self-determination theory and the facilitation of intrinsic motivation, social development and well-being. *American Psychologist*, **55**: 68–78.

Sarason, I.G. (1984). Stress, anxiety and cognitive interference: reactions to tests. *Journal of Personality and Social Psychology*, **46**(4): 929–38.

Seipp, B. (1991). Anxiety and academic performance: a meta-analysis of findings. *Anxiety Research*, **4**: 27–41.

Spielberger, C., Anton, W. & Bedell, J. (1983). The nature and treatment of test anxiety. In M. Zuckerman & C.D. Spielberger (eds), *Emotion and Anxiety: New Concepts, Methods and Applications*. Hillside, NJ: Erlbaum, pp. 317–45.

Sternberg, R.J. (1996). Intelligence and cognitive styles. In S.E. Hampson & A.M. Coleman (eds), *Individual Differences and Personality*. London: Longman.

Sternberg, R.J. (1997). *Thinking Styles*. Cambridge: Cambridge University Press.

Taylor, J.A. (1953). A personality scale of manifest anxiety. *The Journal of Abnormal and Social Psychology*, **48**(2): 285–90.

Zeidner, M. (1998). *Test Anxiety: The State of the Art*. New York & London: Plenum Press.

Index